FREEDOM IN THE MIDST OF A SLAVE SOCIETY

Study & Share this new history with your family & friends!
Edna B. McKenzie

A Documentary Supplement for Courses in the Afro-American Experience

Essays and Commentary by
Edna B. McKenzie
Community College of Allegheny County

THE ASSOCIATED PUBLISHERS, INC.
1407 Fourteenth Street, N.W.
Washington, D.C. 20005

The Associated Publisher, Inc.

1407 14th Street, N.W.
Washington, D.C. 20005

Printed in the United States of America

Library of Congress Cataloging in Publication Data

McKenzie, Edna.
Freedom in the midst of a slave society.

Library of Congress Catalog
Card Number 89-083535

ISBN 0 87498-0038

Pages reproduced in this pamphlet are taken from first editions of listed works which are the property of the author and may be examined by students on special request.

TITLE PAGE

Statue of Freedom on Dome of the Capitol
Erected by a black artisan, Philip Reed, a slave.

FOREWORD

It is my firm conviction that much of the racism in American society may be attributed to an appalling lack of information about the participation of blacks and other minorities in the historic development of this nation.

Students who enroll in United States and Afro-American History classes at Allegheny Campus of CCAC express genuine surprise and sometimes actual shock when assigned readings about the free black population in the pre-Civil War South. They have been permitted to assume that all blacks were slaves for life. Therefore, it is difficult for them to accept information about the progress made by a strong leadership class of black Americans who spread out all over the country and who were not only free but often prosperous and well-educated.

The purpose of this documentary supplement, **Freedom in the Midst,** is to emphasize that there were always men and women, black and white, North and South, who established and maintained pathways to liberty and human dignity. Despite restrictive and repressive legal systems these early freedom fighters achieved and accumulated and they were not powerless. It was largely through their efforts that slavery was finally destroyed.

Seeing is more than believing. Endless questions are raised and fervent search for truth begins with examination of the primary data from which all history should be written and taught.

Hopefully, this pamphlet will increase the ranks of searchers for truth and contribute to a more enlightened view of the total American experience.

Edna B. McKenzie, Ph.D., Chairperson
Black, Minority and Ethnic Studies Department

A MESSAGE TO TEACHERS AND STUDENTS

This second edition of **Freedom in the Midst** is offered as a supplement to comprehensive texts for all secondary levels in the study of American history, black and minority studies, the humanities and related social sciences. The essays are meant to serve as points of departure for lectures, classroom debate, research and library assignments. It is generally agreed by all American scholars that an enormous amount of very important information has been omitted from the standard versions of the American experience. We have expanded this offering to include some facts about black women, the independent black church, the press and some lesser known leaders and achievers.

For examples, Frances Watkins Harper was eloquent and intelligent and every bit as effective as Sojourner Truth on the public platform during the pre-Civil War period; Dr. Martin R. Delaney was certainly as great a hero as Frederick Douglass. Serious examination of the records left by these men and women — especially people like the two who have been ignored by most historians — would probably contribute much toward desegregation of the minds of teachers, students and parents of both races. Blacks and whites need to know more about their shared past in order to secure a more successful future for our multicultural nation.

NOTE: *In order to avoid purchasing notebooks, students are urged to record notes and assignments in the blank areas provided for that purpose throughout this book.*

TABLE OF CONTENTS

THE AFRICAN BACKGROUND

Most Americans are now familiar with the fossil findings of the famous British anthropologists, Mary and L.S.B. Leakey, who have proven that Africa is the birthplace of mankind. Contemporary historians join with other social scientists in constant research and reassessment of Africa's role in world civilization. They are exploding old myths and sweeping away outdated stereotypes about the second largest continent which most traditional writers described in terms of darkness and backwardness.

The work of the late Professor Leo Weiner of Harvard and the late Joel A. Rogers, world traveler and publisher of note, along with modern historians like Basil Davidson and John Henrick Clarke, has greatly influenced the new quest for a more enlightened view. A dedicated cadre of vigorous researchers are attempting to rescue the American public from the devastating consequences of gross ignorance about old world peoples and cultures.

While teaching at Harvard University in 1971, Stanlake Samkange, a native of Rhodesia, wrote an absorbing book, **"The African Saga"** which is used as a major source for the introductory course in Afro-American History on Allegheny Campus. Dr. Samkange wrote:

> *"In answer to those who ask: What has Africa contributed to world progress? We can say that Africa gave birth to man and is man's original home, that the oldest cultures on earth evolved in Africa. It was in Africa that man took the most important steps toward domesticating himself, thus increasing his chances for continuation of his kind."* *

Elementary school textbooks in several major cities now include stories about the rise and fall of glorious medieval African kingdoms, Ghana, Mali, and Songhay. This represents a giant step forward, but it is only the beginning. More important, recent developments in international economics and politics make it clear that students must be presented a broader perspective to be able to cope with the rapidly changing world of today.

* Stanlake Samkange, **The African Saga,** New York, 1971, p.33.

Translation of the above in part: "The Great King, Monomotapa. Very powerful and rich in gold. Several kings are tributary to him. His territory comprises lower Ethiopia. . . . His empire is very large and has a circuit of 2,400 miles. His court is at Zimboae (Zymbabwe). There are women in his guard . . . . He has a great number of them in his army which give great help to the men. He also has a great number of elephants. His subjects are black, brave and swift runners, and he has very fast horses. Idolaters, sorcerers, adulterers, and thieves are severely punished."

The Great King, a portrait of one the rulers of the ancient African kingdom, Zymbabwe. Reprinted with permission from a collection by the late Joel A. Rogers.

TIMBUCTOO OF OLD WAS A WORLD CENTER OF TRADE AND LEARNING

First known picture of Timbuctoo, capital of the mighty Songhay Empire of Africa founded 1490 A.D. Southern portion of the City. (Drawn by Rene Caille, French explorer in 1828).

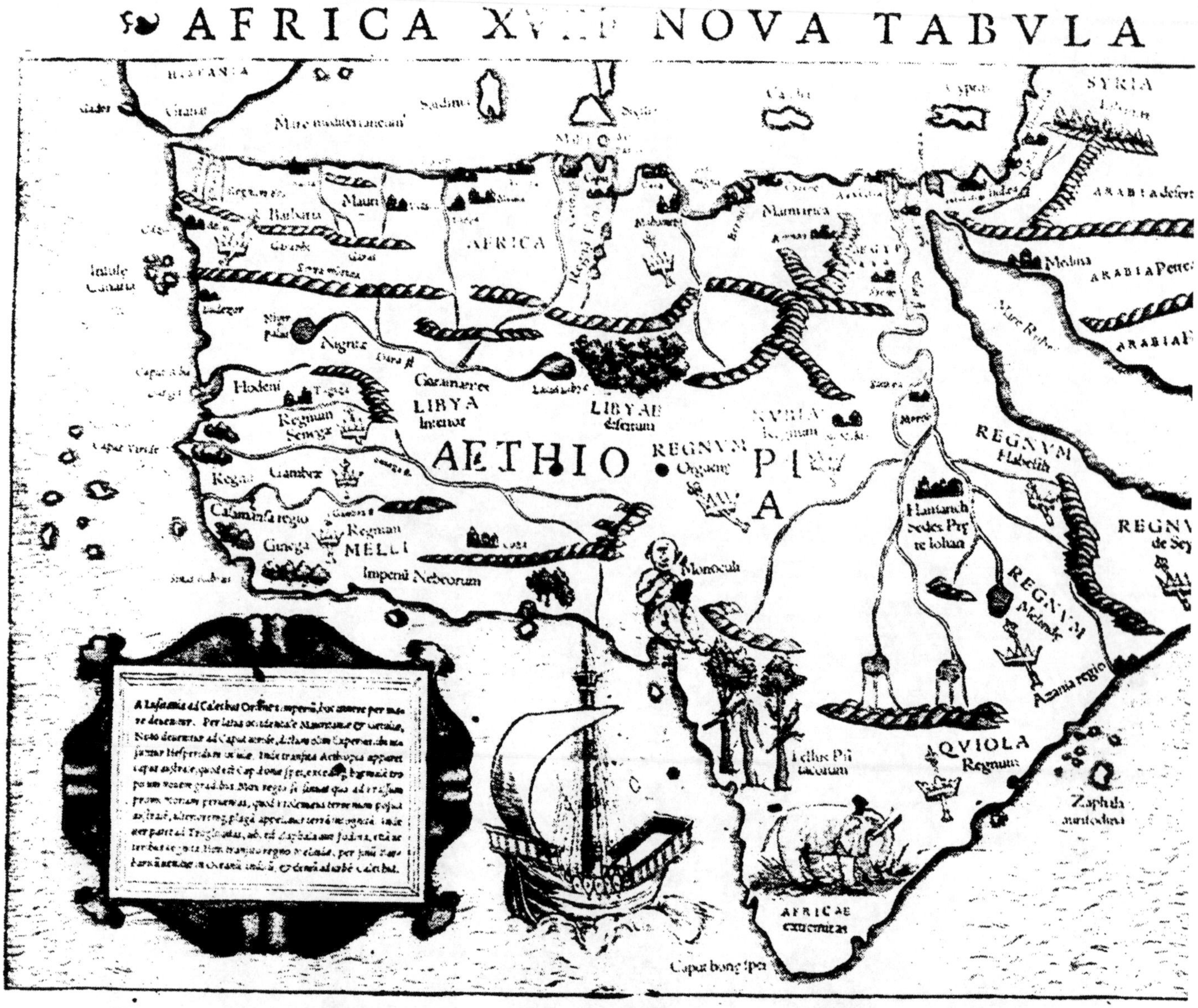

The map above is one of the many on display in the National Museum of Tanzania, in the capital city of Dar es Salaam on the Indian Ocean.

The face of the land changed radically after the military and economic penetration by European empire builders. The ancient kingdom of Aethiopia was once the most powerful and extensive. See "Africa" bordering on the Mediterrean Sea and "Aegpyt" to the northeast. Also note the Kingdom of Barbara near Hispania to the northwest, later known as the Barbary States with which the United States fought a series of undeclared wars in the late eighteenth and early nineteenth centuries. America fought and negotiated to redeem her citizens from among the many white people who had been sold into slavery in Africa.

OUTLINE FOR STUDY

AFRO-AMERICAN HISTORY I

THE AFRICAN BACKGROUND

A. Name three noted scholars whose research support claims that Africa is the birthplace of mankind.

1. ____________________

2. ____________________

3. ____________________

B. Explain the importance of using primary sources for the study of history. What are secondary sources?

Definition of terms ____________________

____

____

Examples ____________________

____

____

C. What are some of the benefits of using an interdisciplinary approach?

1. ____________________

____

2. ____________________

____

3. ____________________

____

D. Name three African kingdoms which flourished during the period known in Western Civilization as the Dark Ages.

1. ____________________

2. ____________________

3. ____________________

State one important fact about each of the kingdoms. *Example: The University of Sankore was located in the ancient city of Timbuctoo in the Kingdom of Songhay.*

1. ______________________________

2. ______________________________

3. ______________________________

E. Name three scholars who have given us information translated from Arabic sources.

1. ______________________________

2. ______________________________

3. ______________________________

—NOTES—

A TABLE,

Exhibiting the amount of the African portion of the population of the United States, according to the Returns of the several Censuses, with the ratio of increase.

CENSUS OF 1790.

Slaves, - - - - - - - -	697,697
All other persons of colour except Indians, not taxed, - -	59,481

CENSUS OF 1800.

Slaves, - - - - - - - -	896,849
All other persons, as above, - - - - -	110,072

Rate of increase of slaves between 1790 and 1800	2.85442 pr. ct. pr. ann.
Do. do. persons of colour do.	8.5054

CENSUS OF 1810.

Slaves, - - - - - - - -	1,191,364
All other persons of colour, as abvoe, - - - -	186,446

Rate of increase of slaves between 1800 and 1810	3.2838861 pr. ct. pr. ann.
Do. do. persons of colour do. -	6.93854931

CENSUS OF 1820.

Slaves, - - - - - - - -	1,538,128
All other persons of colour, as above, - - - -	233,530

Rate of increase of slaves between 1810 and 1820	2.911
Do. do. persons of colour do. -	2.52534246

Mean ratio of increase of slaves during the whole period of 30 years,	3.0164353
Do. of persons of colour, - - - -	5.9897639

Present rate of increase of slaves, according to the last Census,	2.911
Do. do of free persons of colour -	2.52534246

or a little more than two and a half per cent. per annum.

PATHWAYS TO FREEDOM AND COMMUNITY DEVELOPMENT

Most Americans have been under the impression that emancipation always came as a result of benevolent acts on the part of the former slave masters when, in reality, many were able to save money through their own efforts and purchase their freedom. These free men in turn played an important role in helping fellow blacks gain liberty. It is true that the post-Revolutionary War period was marked by a wave of benevolent emancipations such as is requested in the Kosciuszko testamentary. However, the early nineteenth century economic upsurge drastically increased the demand for workers and tightened the bonds of those in forced labor systems. The situation called for more pragmatic responses from those who were victimized, as well as those who sympathized.

Suits for freedom were more frequent than is generally known. This 1820 document showing "Amos Joseph and other black persons suing for their freedom" (sic) is an example of the type of evidence found in court reports and record books particularly in the more northern regions of Virginia, Maryland, and Washington, D.C.

Self-purchase was practiced throughout the period of slavery. Among early church leaders there are numerous examples of artisans who like Richard Allen, Methodist, and Andrew Bryan, Baptist, used their skills and resources for the benefit of the total black community. After buying their own freedom both these men purchased lots on which meeting houses were erected.

Benjamin Lundy, the noted anti-slavery pioneer and publisher, writes in his journal about meeting a former slave in Texas (then a part of Mexico) during 1833 who had purchased "five or six" houses and a plot of land and provided the best education possible for his children.

THERE WERE NUMEROUS BENEVOLENT EMANCIPATIONS
DURING THE REVOLUTIONARY WAR PERIOD

opinion, so successfully have the seeds of Colonization been sown, that together with the natural advantages of Africa, and with the improvements made by the Colonists, you have planted a standard that all your opposers cannot overthrow.* *

We have some very respectable people among the emigrants from New Orleans. Among them are Messrs. Simpson and Moore; Mr. Finley, it seems, from the advice of his brother, has taken charge of them, and is fixing many of them at Millsburg. * *

In conclusion, permit me to ask the favor of you, gentlemen, to write me, as I shall write you hereafter, as often as I shall find it acceptable to you. You will have the goodness to put me on the list of subscribers to the African Repository.

JAMES BROWN.

THE KOSCIUSZKO FUND.

On the 5th of May, 1798, Kosciuszko, the celebrated Polish General, placed a fund in the hands of Mr. Jefferson, and executed a will as follows:

"I, Thaddeus Kosciuszko, being just on my departure from America, do hereby declare and direct, that, should I make no other testamentary disposition of my property in the United States, I hereby authorize my friend, Thomas Jefferson, to employ the whole thereof in purchasing negroes, from among his own or any others, and giving them liberty in my name, in giving them an education in trade or otherwise, and in having them instructed for their new condition in the duties of morality, which may make them good neighbours, good fathers or *mothers*, husbands or wives, in their duty as citizens, teaching them to be defenders of their liberty and country, and of the good order of society, and in whatsoever may make them happy and useful. And I make the said Thomas Jefferson my Executor of this. (Signed) T. Kosciuszko, 5 May, 1798."

Kosciuszko died October 15, 1817; and Mr. Jefferson refusing to take out letters testamentary under his will, Benjamin Lincoln Lear was appointed Administrator with the will annexed. Under another will, alleged to have been executed by Kosciuszko at Paris, in June 1806, Kosciuszko Armstrong claimed of the Administrator $3,704 out of the funds in his hands. The bill in chancery making the claim was dismissed by the Circuit Court of the District of Columbia for Washington County, because it did not appear that the will of June 1806 had been admitted to probate in either France or the Orphans Court of that County. At February term 1827, this decision was affirmed by the Supreme Court of the United States.*

The validity of the will of May 5, 1798, was denied by the distributees and next of kin of Kosciuszko, and the fund was claimed by them. At January term 1833, the Supreme Court considered the case, and remanded it for further proceedings.†

The case of Armstrong *v.* Lear again came before the Supreme Court, at January term 1834, and was remanded for further proceedings.‡

The following letter in relation to the fund, has recently been written to the Editor of Zion's Herald in Boston:

---

* Armstrong *v.* Lear, Admr. of Kosciuszko, 12 Wheat. 169.
† Estho *et al*, *v.* Lear, Admr. &c., 7 Peters, 130.
‡ 8 Peters, 52.

Reprinted from the October, 1835 African Repository and Colonial Journal, published by the American Colonization Society.

Afro-Americans have always fought for freedom through the courts. The case of Jenny Slew of Ipswich, Mass. in 1766 is often cited as the first recorded victory. The document reproduced here shows black persons suing for their freedom charging illegal importation in 1820.

The Commonwealth of Virginia to
Juſtice of the Peace for the County of.
Greeting.

KNOW you, that we, truſting to your fidelity anc ... in diligently examining whatſoever Witneſſes ſhall come before you, as well on behalf of *Amos & others black persons suing for freedom* Plaintiffs as of *James McMecken* Defendant, in a certain Suit commenced and proſecuted in our *Superior* Court of Ohio, at Wheeling, between the aforeſaid parties,—appoint you our Commiſſioner, to call and cauſe to come before you, on ſuch certain days, and at ſuch places as you ſhall appoint, the Witneſſes aforeſaid, and them diligently examine on the Holy Evangeliſt of Almighty God, or on their ſolemn affirmation, *on the annexed Interrogatories* and ſuch examination into our *said Superior* Court, without delay, you ſhall certify and ſend incloſed, returning then there alſo this Writ. Witneſs William Chapline, jun. Clerk of our ſaid Court, at the Court-houſe aforeſaid, this *21st* day of *August 1820* and in the *45* year of the Commonwealth.

Wm Chapline Jr

Amos Joseph & others black persons suing for their freedom vs James McMecken } *Interrogatories to be put to witnesses as well on the behalf of the Defendant as on the part of the Plaintiffs in this Cause*

1st Were you acquainted with one Richard Wetherhead the former claimant of the Plaintiffs, if so do you know when he removed from the State of Maryland to Rockingham County in this Commonwealth

2d. Did he bring any slaves with him, if so please to state their names and ages as correctly as you can,

3d. Did he or any other person for him, before you, as one of the Commonwealths Justices of the peace for the said County of Rockingham, take the oath prescribed by law respecting the importation of slaves, into this Commonwealth please to state as particularly as possible, by whom such oath was taken, when taken, and whether taken within or

Archives, University of West Virginia Library, Morgantown, W. Va.

THE RT. REV. RICHARD ALLEN

First Bishop of the African Methodist Episcopal Church, known as "Apostle of Freedom". He taught self-help and direct action as a means of progress for blacks.

Founder of Bethel Ame Church in Philadelphia, PA now a national shrine. The property was purchased almost two hundred years ago.

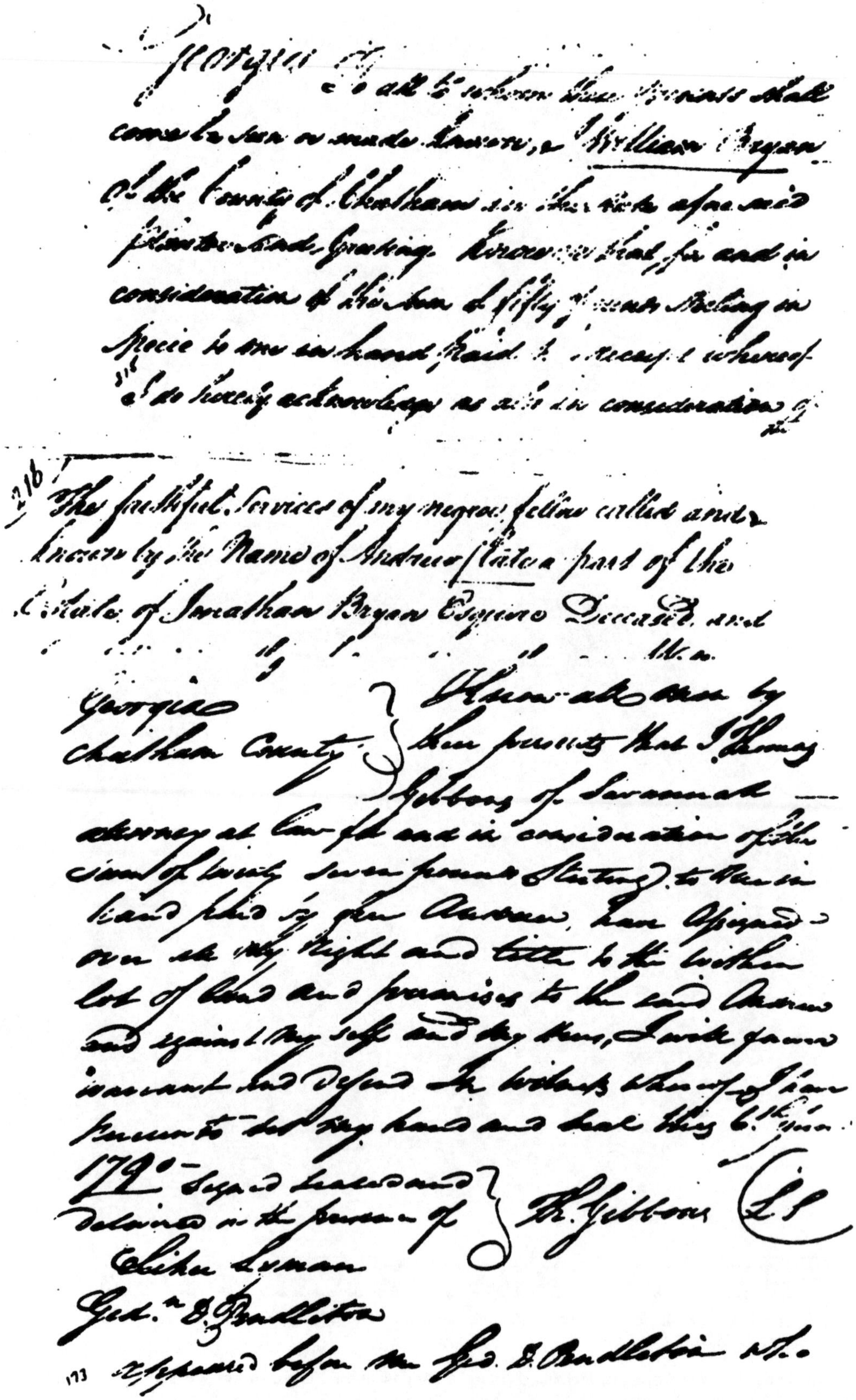
Georgia } To all to whom these presents shall come be seen or made known, I William Bryan of the County of Chatham in the State aforesaid Planter Send Greeting Know ye that for and in consideration of the sum of fifty pounds Sterling in Specie to me in hand paid the receipt whereof I do hereby acknowledge as also in consideration of

216 The faithful Services of my negroe fellow called and known by the Name of Andrew (State a part of the Estate of Jonathan Bryan Esquire Deceased and [illegible]

Georgia
Chatham County } Know all men by these presents that I Thomas Gibbons of Savannah attorney at law for and in consideration of the sum of twenty seven pounds Sterling to me in hand paid by the Andrew have released all my Right and title to the within lot of land and premises to the said Andrew and against my self and my heirs, I will forever warrant and defend In witness whereof I have hereunto set my hand and seal this 6th June 1790 — Signed sealed and delivered in the presence of } Th. Gibbons (LS)
Elisha Lyman
Geo. D. Pendleton
173 Appeared before me Geo. D. Pendleton [illegible]

EARLY CHURCH LEADERS PURCHASED PROPERTY FOR COMMUNITY USE. Like Richard Allen of the Methodist denomination, Andrew Bryan, founder of the African Baptist Church in Savannah, GA purchased his own freedom then bought the lot on which the building was erected. This 1790 deed is recorded in Chatham County, GA.

PROMINENT ABOLITIONIST TELLS ABOUT MEETING SLAVE WHO HAD PURCHASED FREEDOM

The purchase of freedom was always possible, though at times more difficult in certain parts of the slave kingdom. In the above document taken from a travel journal written by an early anti-slavery activist, Benjamin Lundy, he records that on October 29, 1833 he met a former slave "who has purchased the freedom of himself and family."

religious parade is held here to-day. It is a sort of religious invocation to God for preservation from the cholera. There are great apprehensions, among the people, of that terrible disease; and those who can afford it, carry little bags of camphor in their bosoms, to guard against an attack. The state of health, at present, however, is as good as I ever witnessed at any time or place. My own health has become very good.

23d. A row took place yesterday between two of our Northern Americans, or United States people. The victor was taken before the Alcalde, and upon hearing, to-day, was fined ten dollars.—A person who resides on Kimball's Creek, Texas, informs me that there is an abundance of mineral coal in that quarter, similar to that of Pennsylvania, though somewhat more sulphurous.

26th. The merchants with whom I am to go to Monclova, have engaged a team and expect to start in a few days. 28th. A man from Pittsburg, named George Pagan, stole to-day, from my room, a pair of suspenders worth $2. These Mexicans are novices in the arts of thieving, drunkenness and vagabondism, in comparison with these fellows from the North.

29th. I walked out this forenoon with Matthew Thomas, to see the cane patch, grounds, &c., of his father-in-law, Felipe Elua, a black Louisiana creole, who was formerly a slave, but who has purchased the freedom of himself and family. He has resided here twenty-six years, and he now owns five or six houses and lots, besides a fine piece of land near town. He has educated his children so that they can read and write, and speak Spanish as well as French. They are all fine looking, smart black people. He has a sister also residing in Bexar, who is married to a Frenchman. The sugar cane, of which there is a patch of about an acre on Elua's land, looks as well as that which grows in Hayti, and the land is evidently well adapted to it. The frost does not kill the roots of the plant here as it does further north, but the sprouts make their appearance in the spring, so that it is unnecessary to replant it. Besides the cane, we saw some fine looking cotton, a large patch of sweet potatoes, together with beans and other garden vegetables, the property of the same black man, and all in beautiful order.

30th. A merchant named Rubideau,* who arrived here two days since from St. Louis, where I knew something of him in 1820, and whose character and standing is considered good, proposes to buy me a horse and to pay some bills for me, and desires me to accompany him immediately to Monclova. He is a Louisiana French creole, and is now acting as agent for the Missouri fur trading company. He says he knows all about my public career. I have introduced him to my friend Padilla. There is also another person who is going from Monclova to Mexico, that offers to furnish me with money to accompany him. These offers seem certainly to be fair and friendly.

October 1st, 1833. Another month has passed, and I am still here at Bexar.—Another religious procession took place this afternoon. Its object was "to keep away the cholera," as our North Americans here say. I went out with several others to see it. At a particular part of the ceremony all in the procession knelt for a few moments. The same thing is done by the Catholic bystanders, but it is not required of strangers. The latter, however, generally stand and uncover their heads, as a mark of respect.

5th. Our company for Monclova being frightened, by reports of the cholera, have concluded to defer starting for a week or two. Rubideau is willing to go on, but he has an attack of the ague, of which I have undertaken to cure him. To-day some Shawnee and Delaware Indians arrived in town on their way to attack the Camanches. 6th. There is a very cool north wind today. The Mexicans are all blanketed up as they walk abroad.

* Called Robidoux in a subsequent part of the journal.

Document taken from The Life, Travels and Opinions of Benjamin Lundy, Philadelphia: 1847.

THE ENDURING DECISION:
"HERE WE WERE BORN AND HERE WE WILL DIE"

The most influential leaders in the political, economic and social spheres in America agreed very early that the best solution to the problems created by the presence of Afro-Americans was to export those who made up the troublesome free black class. Officers and activists in the American Colonization Society, organized in 1816, included John Marshall, John Randolph, James Madison, James Monroe, Henry Clay, Francis Scott Key, and Bushrod Washington, nephew of the founding father.

The purpose of this society is plainly stated in Article I of its constitution. However, the overwhelming majority of the black population rejected the offer at the outset and continued to oppose the plan. One month after the colonization design was announced leaders of the free blacks called a mass meeting at "Mother" Bethel Church in Philadelphia and announced their determination to stay in America and claim not only freedom, but all the benefits enjoyed by other native citizens.

In a recent historical work, Carol V.R. George analyzed the response of blacks during the first twenty years of the movement, stating:

> *"Such appeals produced some converts; in 1832, 796 Afro-Americans left for their "homeland", the largest group up to that time, thus bringing the total number of emigrants up to 2,638. Since the free Northern black population in 1830 totaled 166,757, it was obvious that only a small percentage were listening to the Society's message."* *

*Carol V.R. George, Segregated Sabbaths, Richard Allen And the Emergence of Independent Black Churches, 1760-1840, New York: 1973, p. 153.

Repeated efforts were made by powerful political groups to remove blacks to Liberia, Mexico, Haiti and various locations in Africa or South America. One of the most vehement spokesmen against such a scheme was Peter Williams, a prominent New York Episcopal clergyman, who declared in 1822:

> *"We are natives of this country, we ask only to be treated as well as foreigners. Not a few of our fathers suffered and bled to purchase its independence; we ask only to be treated as well as those who fought against it. We have toiled to cultivate it and to raise it to its present prosperous condition; we ask only to share equal privileges with those who come from distant lands to enjoy the fruits of our labour. Let these moderate requests be granted, and we need not go to Africa nor anywhere else to be improved and happy. We cannot but doubt the purity of the motives of those persons who deny us these requests, and would send us to Africa to gain what they might give us at home."***

Leslie H. Fishel, Jr., and Benjamin Quarles, eds., **The Negro American: A Documentary History, Glenview, IL, 1967, pp. 146, 147.

Some of the leaders during the late colonial and early national periods in American history were active in the American Colonization Society which was formed in 1816 for the purpose of removing free blacks from their native land.

(No. 9.)

Constitution of the American Colonization Society.

ART. I. This Society shall be called "The American Society for Colonizing the Free People of Colour of the United States."

ART. II. The object to which its attention is to be exclusively directed, is to promote and execute a plan for colonizing (with their consent) the free People of Colour residing in our country, in Africa, or such other place as Congress shall deem most expedient. And the Society shall act, to effect this object, in cooperation with the General Government, and such of the States as may adopt regulations upon the subject.

ART. III. Every citizen of the United States, who shall subscribe these articles, and be an annual contributor of one dollar to the funds of the Society, shall be a member. On paying a sum of not less than thirty dollars, at one subscription, he shall be a member for life.

ART. IV The officers of the Society shall be, a President, Vice-Presidents, a Secretary, a Treasurer, a Recorder, and a Board of Managers, composed of the abovenamed officers, and twelve other members of the Society. They shall be annually elected by the members of the Society, at their annual meeting, on the Saturday preceding New Year's Day, and continue to discharge their respective duties till others are appointed.

ART. V. It shall be the duty of the President to preside at all meetings of the Society, and of the Board of Managers, and to call meetings of the Society, and of the Board, when he thinks necessary, or when required by any three members of the board.

ART. VI. The Vice-Presidents, according to seniority, shall discharge these duties in the absence of the President.

ART. VII. The Secretary shall take minutes of the proceedings, prepare and publish notices, and discharge such other duties as the Board, or the President, or, in his absence, the Vice-President, according to seniority, (when the Board is not sitting,) shall direct. And the Recorder shall record the proceedings and the names of the members, and discharge such other duties as may be required of him.

ART. VIII. The Treasurer shall receive and take charge of the funds of the Society, under such security as may be prescribed by the Board of Managers; keep the accounts, and exhibit a

The above document reprinted from the African Repository and Colonial Journal, January 1835, Vol. XI, No. 1, page 41.

THERE WAS ALSO MASSIVE VIOLENT RESISTANCE TO SLAVERY

It has been too often stated that blacks never engaged in massive, violent resistance to slavery. The official government records shown here indicate major participation by blacks in a costly series of wars involving the United States Army. Most history texts – if they mention the Seminole Wars at all – treat the conflicts as only an Indian uprising, despite the clear testimony of the commanding officer of the national forces during the second conflict. Major General Thomas Jesup reported to the War Department:

> *"This, you may be assured, is a negro, not an Indian war; and if it be not speedily put down, the South will feel the effects of it on their slave populations before the end of the next season."*

Jesup wrote in another communication:

> *"The warriors fought as long as they had life, and such seems to me to be the determination of those who influence their councils – I mean the leading negroes."*

This document also provides additional evidence of villages made up of all black inhabitants. There are various other sources which tell of runaways who maintained their own communities in such forest regions as the Dismal Swamp or mountain areas like Blount's Fort in the Carolinas, Virginia, Georgia and Florida.

SLAVERY NOT ALWAYS FOR LIFE IN SOME STATES

Indenture and term slavery continued through the Civil War period as may be seen in a cursory examination of fugitive slave records in the National Archives in Washington, D.C. Petitions to district courts are noted which complain that runaways still owe a certain number of years to complete their terms of service, indicating they were not considered slaves for life.

The Anthony Williams document is significant because it proves that the two men agreed and formalized their bargain on July 3, 1792. Though a slave, according to several other documents about this same case acquired by this researcher, Williams appeared in Monongalia County Court in Virginia in 1800 with the agreement and a note from his owner, Mathias Hite, restating the contract. Hite attempted to void the bargain and had Williams jailed. However, a jury determined that the black man was entitled to liberty.

This, you may be assured, is a negro, not an Indian war; and if it be not speedily put down, the south will feel the effects of it on their slave population before the end of the next season.

Unless the army be placed upon a better footing, it will disband; discharges are numerous, and no old soldiers re-enlist. The officers cannot subsist on the miserable pittance now allowed them; they should, upon principles of common justice, be placed on a footing with corresponding grades in the navy. You, sir, will command their gratitude, and render an important service to the country, by taking the lead in this matter.

Assure the President that whatsoever promptness and energy can accomplish shall be done.

With high consideration and respect, I am, sir, your obedient servant,

THOMAS S. JESUP.

Hon. B F. Butler, *Acting Secretary of War, Washington City.*

Headquarters, *Fort Dade, February* 17, 1837.

Sir: I had the honor to receive last night your letter of the 4th ultimo, with a copy of the President's message and the documents accompanying it, for which accept my acknowledgments.

I am waiting most anxiously the movements of the hostile chiefs. The attack on Lieutenant Colonel Fanning has caused me to doubt their sincerity even more than before; for, although I consider myself bound to allow them an opportunity to come in, I place but little reliance on their professions. There would be no difficulty in making peace if they were allowed to remain in the country even as citizens, or individuals subjected to our laws; but many of them prefer death to removal. In all the numerous battles and skirmishes that have taken place, not a single first-rate warrior has been captured, and only [illegible] Indian men have surrendered.

The warriors have fought as long as they had life, and such seems to me to be the determination of [illegible] who influence their councils—I mean the leading negroes. To-morrow, however, will determine the question as to their sincerity. Should they refuse the terms which I have offered, the war must recommence, and there will be little prospect of closing it during the present season.

If I were as well acquainted with the country as the hostile chiefs are, I would undertake to defend it with five hundred men against as many thousand. My last march, as well as the operations of Lieutenant Colonels Foster and Fanning, has demonstrated that we can pursue the enemy into their strongest holds, but we cannot remain there a sufficient length of time to produce any lasting effect upon them.

We may conquer them in time, and may destroy them, it is true; but the war will be a most harassing one, and will retard the settlement and improvement of this country for many years to come. I am not disposed to overrate the difficulties which surround me; but, in communicating with you, it would

---

Volusia, *Florida, December* 5, 1836.

Sir: I was not able to obtain the means of transportation for even ten days' supply of subsistence and forage for the troops under my command at Tampa Bay until the 17th of last month; the mules sent for that purpose from New Orleans were entirely unbroken, and it was not until the 27th that I was able to commence the march on the Withlacoochee. When the troops had been put in motion, I received intelligence that Governor Call had reached that river on the 13th, had swept the cove, and had, after driving the Indians, marched across the country to this post.

I immediately countermanded the march of the troops, and, putting myself at the head of four hundred mounted men, on the 27th ultimo pushed through the country and joined the governor last night.

On the 3d instant my spy company succeeded in capturing an Indian near the Ocklawaha river, from whom I received information of the situation of a village, inhabited by negroes, on the lake in which the river has its source. I detached Lieutenant Colonel Cawlfield, of the Alabama twelve months' volunteers, with orders to burn the village and capture or destroy its inhabitants.

The result of the expedition was the destruction of the village and the capture of forty-one negroes. The service was performed in the most prompt and handsome manner.

I have not yet received a return of the troops at this post, nor of the supplies; but I hope to have both to-day. After which, I shall be able to form some idea of the operations proper to be undertaken.

I have not yet received the instructions from the War Department to assume the command in Florida. They were forwarded, *via* Fort Clinch, to Tampa Bay; and the messenger had not arrived there when I took my departure for this place. Governor Call, however, has given me a copy of them, and will turn over the command to me as soon as the necessary returns can be prepared.

I have the honor to be, sir, your obedient servant,

THOMAS S. JESUP, *Major-General, Commanding Army of the South.*

Brigadier General R. Jones, *Adjutant General, Washington City.*

Headquarters Army of the South, *Volusia, Florida, December* 9, 1836.

American State Papers, Military Affairs, 24th and 25th Congress, March 1, 1837 to March 1, 1838; Washington, D.C., Vol. VII, pp. 821, 832.

Memorandum of agreement made between Negro Anthony
and Matthias Hite. Witness that the said Anthony doth
agree to Serve the said Hite faithfully and truly for
Sand during the Term of Eight Years, during all which
Anthony faithfully shall serve him, he shall not absent
himself from his said Masters services without his leave
he shall not make use of his masters Creatures or any
of his property without his leave. Neither run away
during said Term. In Consideration whereof the Said
Hite doth agree at the Experation of the Term aforesaid
to free the said Anthony from Slavery, against the Time
aforesaid of said Hite his heirs and assigns or any other person
or persons whatsoever, also give unto the said Anthony
One horse, Saddle, and Bridle of the Value of Ten pounds
In Compliance of all and every the above articles the
parties do hereby bind themselves their Heirs &c in the
Penal Sum of Fifty [illegible] and in testimony whereof
the parties have interchangeably set their hands and seals
this 3d day of July 1792.

Sealed and delivered in presence of
A Smith
James Patterson

Signed
Anthony his mark Williams (LS)
Mathias Hite (LS)

Archives, University of West Virginia Library, Morgantown, WV.

TYPICAL TRANSACTIONS IN A SLAVE SOCIETY

Typical transactions such as the two printed receipts for slave purchases form the basis for continuing controversy about what should be described as a "normal" situation in the American South. Note that in Lynchburg, Virginia, a "sound and healthy" man was sold for twenty-eight hundred dollars in 1863. During 1860 the price for a similar sale in Richmond was eleven hundred and ten dollars.

In what appears to be 1830, a pass to New Orleans was issued to a slave from his master requesting the "harbour master and collector of customs of that place would therefore please not molest him."

Slave families were apparently stable in some places and marriages were recognized and legalized if acts passed by legislative assemblies are accepted as valid. Alabama required that the assembly pass a separate bill for each emancipation and observed that in 1830 emancipations of slave families were recorded. In section 6: "Thomas and Clary, his wife" and their children were freed. In section 7: "John and also his wife, a female slave by the name of Delilah" are granted liberty.

Jonathan Walker, a New England abolitionist, like numerous others, paid a high price for his involvement in the cause of freedom for blacks. **"The Branded Hand"**, published in 1846, the story of the cruel treatment he suffered because he could not turn his back on the less fortunate, is one of the most moving narratives of the era.

Samuel I. Cabbel, a member of a prominent Virginia family, was anxious to to provide for the care of the slave woman, Mary Barnes, who lived with him as his wife. In 1851 he directed that all the income from his property, hire of slaves and other investments be used for her and her children. A later will, dated May 9, 1859, listed the children and provided for their immediate emancipation and for cash awards of from $2,000 to $3,500 for each of them.

Kanawha County Court Records, Archives, University of West Virginia, Morgantown, WV.

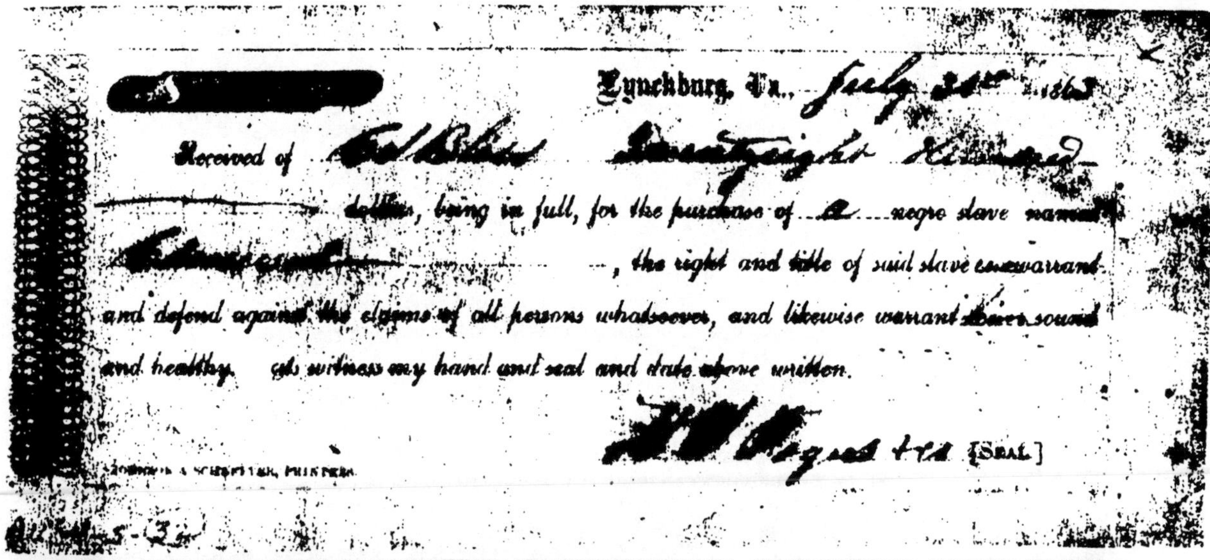

Lynchburg, Va., July 31st 186[illegible]

Received of [illegible] [illegible] hundred dollars, being in full, for the purchase of a negro slave named [illegible], the right and title of said slave I warrant and defend against the claims of all persons whatsoever, and likewise warrant him sound and healthy. As witness my hand and seal and date above written.

[illegible] [SEAL]

BILL-OF-SALE

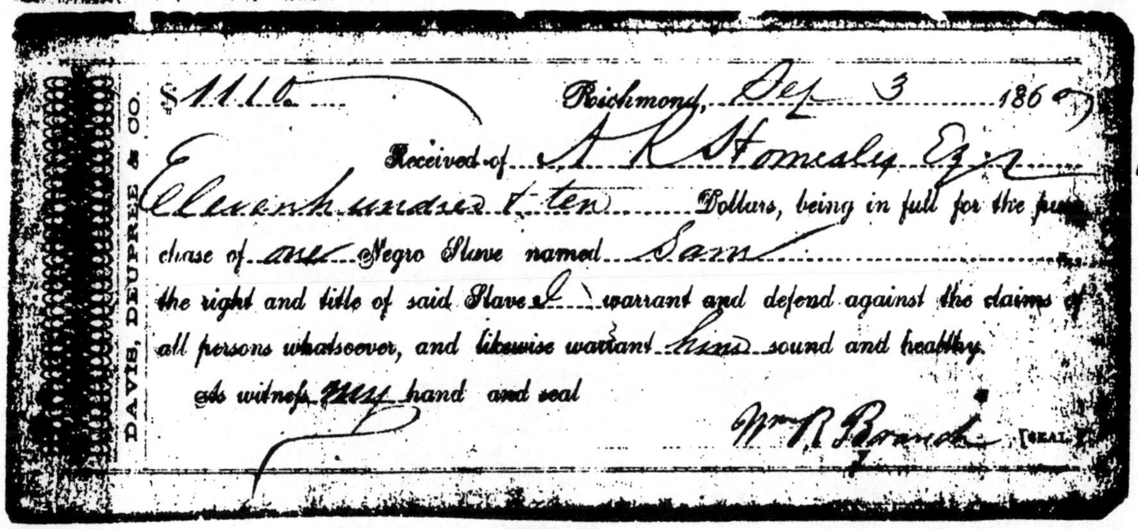

DAVIS, DEUPREE & CO.

$1110 Richmond, Sep 3 1860

Received of A K [illegible] Esq Eleven hundred & ten Dollars, being in full for the purchase of one Negro Slave named Sam the right and title of said Slave I warrant and defend against the claims of all persons whatsoever, and likewise warrant him sound and healthy.

As witness my hand and seal

Wm R Branch [SEAL]

BILL-OF-SALE

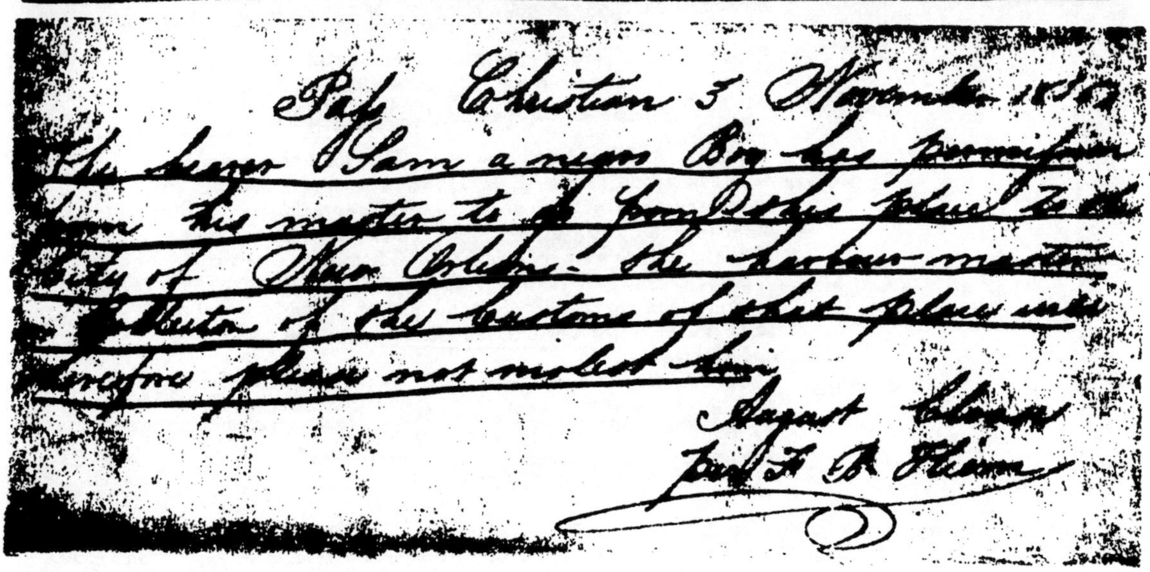

Pass Christian 5 November 18[illegible]

The bearer Sam a negro Boy has permission from his master to [illegible] place to the City of New Orleans. The harbour master [illegible] of the customs of that place [illegible] therefore please not molest him.

August [illegible]

per F. B. [illegible]

PASS

Slave documents from archives in Virginia State Library, Richmond, VA and Atlanta University, Atlanta, GA.

1830. 68

cipate a male slave by the name of [redacted] also a fe-
slave by the name of [redacted]

J B Mansen. Sec. 26. And be it [redacted] enacted, That John Bati-sen of the county of Mobile, be, and he is hereby auth- emancipate two female slaves by the name of Nanc- Catharine.

J Marast. Sec. 27. And be it further enacted, That John Marast county of Greene, be, and he is hereby authorized to e- pate a certain [redacted].

Sally Phagan emancipated. Sec. 28 And be it further enacted, That Sally Pha- woman of color, who has been purchased by contribu- sundry citizens of the county of Madison, for the purp- emancipating, be, and she is hereby forever freed from bo- and slavery, reserving at the same time the rights of ci-

Bond to be given. and upon condition that security shall be given to the judge the County Court of said county in the sum of one hundred lars, conditioned, that she shall not become a public char-. [redacted]

AN ACT

To authorize the emancipation of certain slaves therein named.

Section 1. Be it enacted by the Senate and House of Representatives of the State of Alabama in General Assembly con-

Achelus Pope authorised to emancipate slave. That Achelus Pope [redacted] here by [redacted] a certain coloured man by the name of Silas.

Dav'd Brewton authorized to emancipate slave. [redacted] further enacted, That David Brew- the county of Madison be, and he is hereby authoriz- emancipate a certain man slave by the name of Dane.

Executor of Richard Rapier. Sec. [redacted] Thomas Simpson, executors of the last will and testament Richard Rapier, deceased, of the county of Lauderdale be, they are hereby authorized to emancipate a certain male [redacted]

John Moye, Sec. 4. [redacted] enacted, That Jason Moye of county of Baldwin be, and he is [redacted] authorized to emancipate a certain [redacted]

A C Thompson. Sec. 5. [redacted] Thom- of the county of Franklin be, and he is hereby authoriz- emancipate a [redacted]

S Brown, Sec. 6. And be it further enacted, That Stephen Brown county of Clarke be, and he is hereby authorized to em- cipate certain slaves, to wit: [redacted] and Noah, [redacted] children of the said Thomas [redacted]

Executors of R Thompson. Sec. 7. And be it further enacted, That the executors of Robert Thompson, deceased, of Madison county, be, and they are hereby authorized to emancipate a certain male slave by the name of John and also his wife, a female slave by the name of Delilah, the property of said Robert Thompson, deceased.

A H Bodin, Sec. 8. And be it further enacted, That Alexander Henry Bodin, of the county of Mobile, be, and he is hereby authorized to emancipate two certain female slaves, to wit: E-tras- and Mercide.

Dan'l Reed, Sec. 9. And be it further enacted, That Daniel Reed, a free man of colour of the [redacted] by [redacted] a certain mulatto [redacted] the name of George Reed.

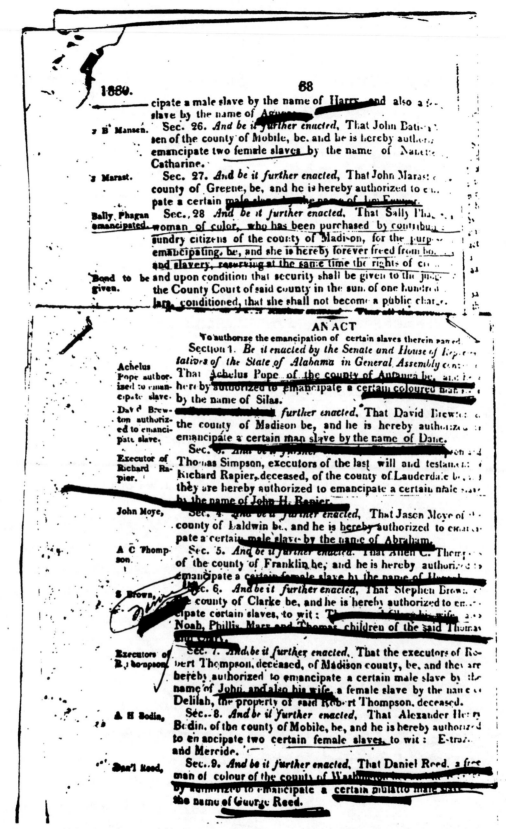

An act of the state legislature was required to free slaves in Alabama. Shown above is record of 1830 session in which twenty-eight acts of emancipation were passed. In section 6 "Thomas and Clary, his wife" and their children are freed. In section 7 "John and also his wife, a female slave by the name of Delilah" are given legal freedom. Acts of Alabama, 1830; Tutwiler Collection, Birmingham Public Library, Birmingham, Alabama.

TRIAL AND IMPRISONMENT

OF

JONATHAN WALKER,

AT PENSACOLA, FLORIDA,

FOR

AIDING SLAVES TO ESCAPE FROM BONDAGE.

WITH AN

APPENDIX,

CONTAINING A SKETCH OF HIS LIFE.

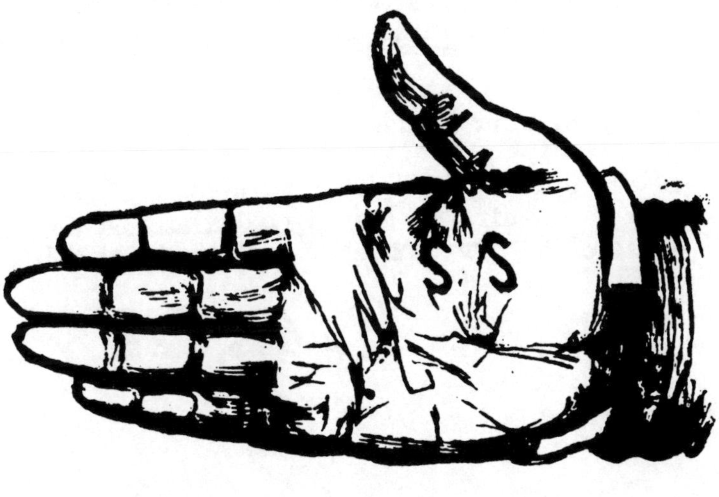

"All things whatsoever ye would that men should do unto you, do ye even so unto them. For this is the law and the prophets."

BOSTON:
PUBLISHED AT THE ANTI-SLAVERY OFFICE
25 Cornhill.
1846.

TESTATOR 231

Cobbel, Samuel I.

RESIDENCE

County of Kanawha, State of Virginia.

DATE OF WILL

November 24, 1851.

DATE OF PROBATE

LEGATEE RELATIONSHIP

Slaves

DEVICE

PERSONAL

All slaves over 21, to be hired out for six years, and then granted freedom. Slaves under 21 employed until they become twenty six and then emincipation. Each slave a suit of clothes and $100 when freed.

LEGATEE RELATIONSHIP

Mary Barnes Negro Woman

DEVICE

PERSONAL

Immediate emincipation after my death. Income from investments, property, and hire of slaves shall be invested in stock proceeds, to Mary Barnes.

LEGATEE RELATIONSHIP

Children of Mary Barnes Children of Negro Woman

DEVICE

Immediate emincipation after my death. Income from investments property, and hire of slaves shall be invested in stock proceeds, to children of Mary Barnes. Residue to children of Mary Barnes.

WITNESSES

Spicer Patrick, Wm. Gillison, and Wm. F. Goshorn.

REFERENCE

Will Book II Page 132

BLACKS AND WHITES TOGETHER ESTABLISHED A MUTUALLY BENEFICIAL SELF-HIRE SYSTEM

The stability of slavery was immeasurably weakened and continually threatened by a system of self-hire which permitted slaves to bargain with owners and hirers for their wages and conditions of work. Self-hire derived primarily from a larger network in which owners hired out their laborers and artisans to other employers for a wide variety of tasks ranging from a one-day job on a neighboring plantation to yearly contracts in industrial plants. The difference between the two practices was crucial. In the hiring out system the owner received the paycheck, but the self-hired worker received his own wages and turned over a stipulated kickback to his partner-master.

Self-hire was widely practiced and many persons progressed from it to the free black class. Others, however, remained in that status because they were hindered by circumstances beyond their control or because they preferred a situation of de facto freedom based on financial independence, which gave them control over their daily existence and helped provide a higher quality of life for themselves and their families.

Documents in this study instrument present evidence of the use of self-hire in Virginia, Washington, D.C., Tennessee, Kentucky, and Georgia and Louisiana. There is abundant evidence in legal reports of appellate cases and in numerous county courthouses throughout the South. The 1850 Georgia law, printed as an example of the language used, clearly implies that those lawmakers considered self-hire a dangerous threat to the status quo and found it expedient to impose an unusually high fine for each offense.

Pages from Josiah Henson's narrative reveal how this highly-skilled carpenter was able to save a large sum of money to bargain for freedom. Paul Jennings was responsible for his own living arrangements while he purchased his liberty on the installment plan, according to the document signed by Daniel Webster. John Edward Bruce, noted journalist of Washington, D.C., writes about his mother who was permitted to "hire her own time."

LAWS DID NOT ALWAYS REFLECT REALITY IN TENNESSEE AND VIRGINIA

Evidence of collaboration between whites and blacks to circumvent unjust laws suggest widespread usage of self-hire and the apprentice system. Slaves were paid for their labor and often lived in a state of de facto freedom.

"In Savannah, according to the account of public buildings given in Sherwood's Gazetteer of Georgia, 2d edition, 1829, page 158, "there are two meeting-houses for Africans; one of which has more than *two thousand* church members attached to the congregation."

"Yet (to use the words of an able writer in that region), every church has a portion of its galleries set apart for the accommodation of the slaves. Here they resort, and listen to the word of God, and partake with their masters and mistresses, and under the same benedictions, of the holy sacrament."

EMANCIPATION.

Mr. ISAAC NOYES, a gentleman residing, we believe, in the State of Virginia, informed TWENTY-FIVE of his adult slaves, on the first of January last, that they were at liberty to work for themselves exclusively; and that, if they would continue in his employ, he would pay them the wages which were received by white men for the same services. He also gave them to understand that he abandoned all right of property in them, and designed to do what he could, under the existing laws, to instruct their minds and improve their hearts. He is now paying them from fifty cents to one dollar a day,

"This is all," says the Cincinnati Journal, "with a design prospectively to their final manumission here, when it can be done without violation of the statute; or their removal to Africa, if they prefer it, whenever a way opens favorable to its accomplishment. Four children of this individual have, within a few years, become hopefully pious; together with a younger brother, who was part owner of the slaves. Eleven of the liberated slaves have, within the same time, professed a hope in the Saviour."

The Rev. FREDERICK A. ROSS, in a letter to President Young, dated Kingston, Tenn., February 6, 1835, states that the letter of the latter gentleman, on Slavery, had brought to determination (his) views on "slavery." This determination is announced as follows:

"My last Will and Testament, as to these servants, is to be fulfilled in conformity with—Measures of Emancipation determined on, in reference to my slaves, January, 1835. The State of Tennessee forbids the manumission of slaves within its limits. But I can effect a virtual emancipation in this State, by adopting the apprentice system. This system is, in my view, better for the servant than immediate manumission. Its results secure, also, as far as may be possible, the interests of the community into which the liberated slave is to enter. For, during this trial of the servant, he has his master's protection from imposition and injury, to both of which he might be exposed were he immediately set free. He has the certainty of employment and support—a most important certainty to the poor laborer, and more especially to the free black laborer. He is gradually qualified for perfect legal emancipation. He has the wages of the free man He may lay up a little capital with which to begin life, when he must take care of himself. And, while he is thus shielded, secured in employment, acquiring habits of self-government, and paid for his labor, the community is preserved as much as possible from the sudden introduction of those unprepared for freedom, and protected from the entrance of the utterly undeserving. In accomplishing these ends, I think I comply with the word of God, towards the servant and to society.

"With this view of the subject, I have determined on the apprentice system in the following form:

"I have twenty-one slaves. Ten of these slaves are over, and eleven are under, twenty-one years of age. From this time until the first January eighteen hundred and forty, which will be five years, I shall place those over twenty-one on the trial of their freedom in all respects, except that they will be under my authority. As many as may be employed by me, I shall pay full wages, and treat as free domestic servants. Those not retained in my service, will be permitted to hire themselves

The African Repository and Colonial Journal, May, 1835, Vol. XI, p. 144.

be eligible to the office of State's Attorney or Solicitor General in any Judicial Circuit in this State, who has not been a resident of the District for one year immediately preceding the time of the election.

SECTION 2. *Be it further enacted by the authority aforesaid*, That all laws and parts of laws militating against this act be and the same are hereby repealed.

Approved, January 17, 1850.

AN ACT to repeal an act approved on the 23d December, 1835, entitled an act to authorize and empower the Surveyor General to record all plats of surveys made on head rights before granting the same.

SECTION 1. *Be it enacted by the Senate and House of Representatives of the State of Georgia in General Assembly met, and it is hereby enacted by the authority of the same*, That the above recited act be and the same is hereby repealed, and that the Surveyor General shall not be required to record any plats of surveys on head rights until the granting of the same.

SECTION 2. *And be it further enacted by the authority aforesaid*, That all laws and parts of laws militating against this act, be and the same are hereby repealed.

Approved, February 11, 1850.

AN ACT to levy and collect a tax for each of the political years 1850 and 1851, and thereafter.

SECTION 1. *Be it enacted by the Senate and House of Representatives of the State of Georgia in General Assembly met, and it is hereby enacted by the authority aforesaid*, That an act entitled an act to levy and collect a tax for each of the political years eighteen hundred and forty-eight and nine, passed by the last General Assembly, be and the same is hereby re-enacted and made of force for the political years 1850 and 1851, and for each year thereafter till repealed.

SECTION 2. *And be it further enacted*, That each and every male citizen between the ages of twenty-one and sixty, be taxed annually the sum of twenty-five cents only.

SECTION 3. *And be it further enacted*, That each and every free negro or free person of color in this State, between the ages of eighteen and fifty, shall be taxed annually the sum of five dollars.

SECTION 4. *And be it further enacted*, That from and after

the first day of March, 1850, each negro or person of color nominally a slave who by any contract or bargain and sale, or pretended bargain and sale, after the date aforesaid, may be held or owned by any white person, said negro or person of color not being over sixty years of age or valueless from decrepitude or disease, shall be taxed one hundred and fifty dollars, and every person when making his or her return shall state on oath what negro or negroes he or she holds in the right of and for the benefit of such negro, and for each and every negro so held, shall pay the tax of one hundred and fifty dollars as above.

SECTION 5. *And be it further enacted*, That from and after the first day of March, all owners or hirers of slaves who shall permit said slave or slaves to hire his or her or their time, from said owners or hirers, at any period during the year, shall pay a tax of one hundred dollars on each and every slave so hiring his or her or their own time: *Provided*, That the giving in said slave or slaves as taxable property to tax assessors by said owner or hirer, shall in no instance be used as evidence against said owner or hirer in an indictment under the existing laws of this State to permit said hiring: *Provided*, That nothing in this section shall operate in the city of Savannah to prevent porters, laborers or others, from working out under the ordinances of said city.

SECTION 6. *And be it further enacted*, That a tax of thirty-one and a quarter cents shall be paid by the Memphis Branch Railroad for each and every hundred dollars of the stock of said road, to be returned and paid into the Treasury in the same manner and at the time required by law in relation to tax on the capital stock of banks, with the same penalty in case of failure.

SECTION 7. *And be it further enacted*, That each President of the different banking companies in this State be and they and each of them shall return on oath the amount of circulation they have out in bills, checks, drafts, or other evidences of debt under the denomination of five dollars, not authorized by law, and that they pay a tax of ten per cent. on the largest amount of illegal circulation in circulation at any time within one year next before making such return.

SECTION 8. *And be it further enacted*, That a tax of fifty cents is hereby imposed on each sulkey and buggy, a tax of one dollar on every rockaway coach or close carriage, a tax of four dollars on each two horse stage, a tax of six dollars on each stage working over two horses, and a tax of ten dollars on each omnibus.

SECTION 9. *And be it further enacted*, That each and every agent of any foreign bank or individual residing in another State, doing business in this State, shall, on or before the first Monday in each and every year, make a return on oath to the Treasurer of this State of the highest amount of loans

The Georgia legislature wrote numerous laws to prevent slaves from hiring their own time. The practice was evidently spreading in 1850 when the lawmakers found it necessary to impose a tax of "one hundred dollars on each and every slave so hiring his, or her or their own time."

Numerous slaves were so highly skilled they were able to negotiate pay for their work. Owners who collaborated in the system of self-hire considered the system mutually beneficial. Henson was a master carpenter.

TRUTH STRANGER THAN FICTION.

FATHER HENSON'S STORY

OF

HIS OWN LIFE.

WITH AN INTRODUCTION

BY MRS. H. B. STOWE.

BOSTON:
JOHN P. JEWETT AND COMPANY.
CLEVELAND, OHIO:
HENRY P. B. JEWETT.
1858.

my money; that with my horse and my pass I was pretty independent of him already, and he had better make up his mind to do what was really inevitable, and do it with a good grace. By such arguments as these, Mr. Frank not only induced him to think of the thing, but before long brought him to an actual bargain, by which he agreed to give me my manumission papers for four hundred and fifty dollars, of which three hundred and fifty dollars were to be in cash, and the remainder in my note. My money and my horse enabled me to pay the cash at once, and thus my great hope seemed in a fair way of being realized.

Some time was spent in the negotiation of this affair, and it was not until the ninth of March, 1829, that I received my manumission papers in due form of law. I prepared to start at once on my return to Kentucky; and on the tenth, as I was getting ready, in the morning, for my journey, my master accosted me in the most friendly manner, and entered into conversation with me about my plans.

An example of the self-hire contract in which slave agrees to repay price of freedom on installment plan, in Washington, D.C. where free blacks outnumbered slaves at a ratio of four to one in 1850.

Schomberg Collection, New York Public Library

Mar: 19. 1847.—
I have paid $120 for
the Freedom of Paul
Jennings— He
agrees to work out the
sum, at 8 dollars a
month, to be found
with board, clothes
& washing— to begin
when we return from
the country— His
freedom papers I give
to him; they are
recorded in this District.
Danl Webster
Washington.

PAGE & FLETCHER
AGENTS FOR
PAGE, KIDDER & FLETCHER
DISTILLERS OF
COAL TAR
AND REFINERS OF
COAL TAR PRODUCTS
10 Warren Street N.Y.

Page & Fletcher.
1302 Penna' Ave. Republican Bld'g
Washington. 18

30 ... "A sketch of my life"

John Edward Bruce was born in Piscataway Maryland February 22nd 1856. Was owned by major Harvey Griffin who served in the war of 1812. he with his mother obtained their freedom one year before the breaking out of the war of the rebellion and came direct to washington city on foot. his father was sold to Georgia when he was three years of age and ~~this~~ he does not know whether he is alive or dead never having heard from him since he was ~~sold~~. we shall now let him tell his own story... I never knew a fathers care nor Do I ever ~~Remember~~ Remember seeing my father My mother was a slave and a hard working one at that after my father was sold My master Gave my mother Permission to work for herself Provided she gave him one half she worked for which she agreed to do. she then obtained a situation as cook in the largest tavern in the village owned and kept by a man Named Ahent. she did not stay there long because the man brute threatened to whip her in one of his drunken sprees. Fort washington is situated about 1 mile from Piscataway on the Merrimac River, My mother worked in the garrison awhile and then she carried on a little business for herself by selling pies

The John Edward Bruce Papers, Schomberg Collection, New York Public Library.

BLACK WOMEN ON THE FIRING LINE

Black women have always been on the firing line in the fight to end oppression and exploitation. They fought in many ways, side by side with the men, throughout the American experience. During the late colonial period in the heat of the conflict with England, Jenny Slew won her liberty in the New England Court, Lucy Terry began the attack on segregated schools, Sarah Allen organized benevolent societies in Philadelphia and Phylis Wheatley exploded the myth of mental inferiority.

The lives of Harriet Tubman, the "Moses" of her people, and Sojourner Truth, a roving messenger whose common sense warnings against the evils of slavery stirred the conscience of the world, have been widely publicized. But there were many others whose achievements merit a place in the history books.

One of the most outstanding women of the late ante-bellum and post-Civil war period was Frances Ellen Watkins Harper, best known for her work as a full-time lecturer for the Maine Anti-Slavery Society. Before she was twenty years old she published her first volume, **"Autumn Leaves"** and her second book, **"Poems on Miscellaneous Subjects"**, printed in Philadelphia in 1854, sold more than 10,000 copies in the first five years and was reprinted several times. Her novels and newspaper features received high praise for their universal appeal.

Born of free parents in Baltimore, Maryland, Frances Harper spent much of her life as an educator. She was trained in the famous Watkins School for free blacks operated by her uncle, William Watkins. After the Civil War she was among the first of the teacher corps who volunteered to instruct the freedmen. Her addresses demonstrate her far-sightedness for she expressed deep concern for women's rights and the plight of children, and she was a faithful worker in the Women's Christian Temperance Union. In one of her most profound statements she expressed this view of the national future:

> *"I hold that between the white people and the colored people there is a community of interest and the sooner they find it out the better it will be for both parties."*

In February, 1965, the black citizens of San Francisco gathered at the grave site of Mary Ellen Pleasant to place a new marker and a modern sculpture commemorating her work as the "Mother of Civil Rights in California". Born a slave in Georgia, Mrs. Pleasant gained her freedom and moved to Boston where she married a wealthy Cuban, Alexander Smith, a serious abolitionist. After his death she remarried, but she kept her promise to use funds from the Smith estate to fight against slavery. She met John Brown in Windsor, Canada, and gave him $30,000 to further his plans for a massive slave rebellion.* Her home was known as a refuge for fugitive slaves.

Mary Ellen Pleasant arrived in California along with the gold seekers and she accumulated a considerable fortune running a boarding house. She was a leader in the fight to expand legal rights for blacks and in 1864 she won a judgment against the street car company in San Francisco for discrimination on a public accommodation.

After Reconstruction when terrorist groups determined to rob blacks of the rights guaranteed in the Fourteenth and Fifteenth Constitutional Amendments, a courageous young woman, Ida B. Wells, launched a vigorous campaign to outlaw lynching. She was born in Holly Springs, Mississippi, where she received her early education. While still a teenager she began teaching and writing and became co-owner of the Free Press, a newspaper in Memphis, Tennessee. Because she printed bold statements condemning town leaders who offered no protection for Afro-Americans, a mob destroyed her business and threatened her life. Escaping to the North, she immediately stepped up her lecture campaign and travelled in Europe to involve the international community in forcing America to live up to her established principles of human rights. She married a Chicago publisher and became a leader in civic and social affairs. She was one of the signers of the first call to establish the National Association for the Advancement of Colored People. A large housing project located in Chicago is named in her honor.

*Manuscript, Mary Ellen Pleasant, by Sue Bailey Thurman, 1949; San Francisco African American Historical and Cultural Society, Inc.

Black women began to enter the professions before the Civil War was over and by the end of the Nineteenth Century they were successful lawyers, doctors, dentists, journalists and educators.

Dr. Hallie Tanner Johnson was born in 1863, daughter of the Rev. and Mrs. Benjamin T. Tanner, a family which had been counted among the free black population since the census of 1800. Hallie Tanner graduated with honor from Women's Medical College in Philadelphia and became the resident physician at Tuskegee Institute. She was required to pass the state examination before she could begin her work and she thus became the first female to practice medicine in Alabama. She established a nurses' training center which received national commendation. She died during 1902, according to a well-known writer, G.F. Richings, whose book, **Evidences of Progress Among Colored People,** was published in 1903. Dr. Johnson was the wife of an AME minister and the sister of the internationally-renowned Pittsburgh painter, Henry O. Tanner.

A strong, noble woman, Mrs. Sarah Orr Clark, working for six dollars a month, purchased the freedom of her brilliant niece, Mrs. Fanny Jackson Coppin, who dedicated her life to the pursuit of freedom from ignorance. Fanny Jackson was born a slave in Washington, D.C. in 1836. After her liberation she was sent to live with another aunt in New Bedford, Massachusetts, where she began her education at the age of fourteen. The young woman worked and studied with such steadfast devotion she won the admiration of prominent citizens of both races. She received financial aid from the George H. Calvert family of Rhode Island and a scholarship from Bishop Daniel A. Payne of the African Methodist Episcopal Church. She attended Oberlin College in Ohio where she excelled in mathematics and the classics and was employed as a teacher before her graduation in 1865. Her reputation as an outstanding teacher was recognized and Oberlin faculty recommended her to the Institute for Colored Youth in Philadelphia. This school, founded in 1837, is now Cheyney State College, the oldest black college in the United States.

Miss Jackson served as teacher and administrator for thirty-five years using her vision and ability to greatly expand both the academic and vocational programs of the college. She married the Rev. Levi J. Coppin who later became an AME bishop and she spent the last decade of her life as a missionary in Africa where her husband was stationed.

FRANCES ELLEN WATKINS HARPER
1825-1911

Memorial Services

IN HONOR OF

MARY ELLEN PLEASANT, 1812-1904

MOTHER OF CIVIL RIGHTS IN CALIFORNIA

FRIEND OF JOHN BROWN

FRIDAY, FEBRUARY 12, 1965

2 O'CLOCK P.M.

TULOCAY CEMETERY

COOMBSVILLE ROAD AND SILVERADO TRAIL

NAPA, CALIFORNIA

UNDER THE AUSPICES OF

THE SAN FRANCISCO NEGRO HISTORICAL

AND CULTURAL SOCIETY

1869-1931

IDA B. WELLS-BARNETT.

DR. HALLIE TANNER JOHNSON.

MRS. FANNY L. JACKSON COPPIN.

THE NATIONAL DILEMMA: SLAVERY IN THE TERRITORIES

Driven to desperation by increasingly vigorous attacks of militant abolitionists, and the petitions of black and white citizens all over the nation calling for laws to prevent the spread of slavery, powerful southern politicians passed a "gag rule" in 1836 to end Congressional debate on the subject of human bondage. John Quincy Adams, former president, then serving in Congress, led a constant battle to repeal the measure, branding it a violation of the First Amendment. "Old Man Eloquent", as Adams was called, prevailed and the restrictive legislation was rescinded in 1844.

With the rapid expansion of the "cotton kingdom" and the national preoccupation with America's "manifest destiny" to overspread the continent, more and more land was acquired by conquest, purchase and diplomacy.

Decades of reform activity dedicated to social betterment climaxed in the intense anti-slavery campaign. The conflicting goals and opinions of the opposing geographic sections were forcefully expressed in the division of the national Democrat and Whig parties and the emergence of new political alliances. Leaders of the Liberty Party were deemed too radical with their demands for immediate abolition. Free-soilers and later, the Republicans, were willing to settle for containment of slavery where it existed. In 1847, David Wilmot of Pennsylvania introduced a bill, which passed in the House, designed to ban slavery in all of the 500,000 square miles taken from Mexico.

The resolutions on the following pages, as they appeared in the Congressional Record, illustrate the divergent postures assumed by northern, western and southern states. Ohio demanded the exclusion of slavery from the Territory of Oregon. South Carolina affirmed:

> *"Resolved unanimously, that the time for discussion by the slaveholding States, as to their exclusion from the territory recently acquired from Mexico has passed."*

The Legislature of New Hampshire took a more radical stand, calling for extinction of slavery in the District of Columbia, its exclusion from Oregon, suppression of the domestic slave trade and resistance to the admission of any more slaves states.

EXCLUSION OF SLAVERY IN TERRITORY TO BE ANNEXED TO THE UNITED STATES.

JOINT RESOLUTIONS

OF THE

LEGISLATURE OF THE STATE OF OHIO,

RELATIVE

To excluding slavery from Oregon Territory, and any other territory which may hereafter be annexed to the United States.

February 15, 1847.
Read, and laid upon the table.

Resolved by the General Assembly of the State of Ohio, That the Senators and Representatives from this State in the Congress of the United States be, and are hereby, respectfully requested to procure the passage of measures in that body providing for the exclusion of slavery from the Territory of Oregon, and also from any other territory that now is or hereafter may be annexed to the United States.

Resolved, That the governor be requested to transmit to each of the Senators and Representatives from this State in the Congress of the United States a copy of the above resolution, to be by them laid before their respective Houses.

WILLIAM P. CUTLER,
Speaker of the House of Representatives.

EDSON B. OLDS,
Speaker of the Senate.

February 8, 1847.

30th Congress, 2d Session. | [SENATE.] | Miscellaneous. No. 51.

RESOLUTIONS

OF THE

LEGISLATURE OF SOUTH CAROLINA,

IN RELATION TO

The "Wilmot Proviso."

February 6, 1849.

Read, and ordered to be printed.

STATE OF SOUTH CAROLINA.

The Joint Committee of the Senate and House of Representatives upon Federal Relations, to whom were referred so much of the governor's message as relates to the agitation of slavery, and sundry resolutions upon the same subject, beg leave to report the following resolution, as expressing the undivided opinion of this legislature upon the Wilmot Proviso, and all similar violations of the great principle of equality which South Carolina has so long and so ardently maintained should govern the action of the States and the laws of Congress upon all matters affecting the rights and interests of any member of this Union:

Resolved, unanimously, That the time for discussion by the slaveholding States, as to their exclusion from the territory recently acquired from Mexico, has passed, and that this General Assembly, representing the feelings of the State of South Carolina, is prepared to co-operate with her sister States in resisting the application of the principles of the Wilmot Proviso to such territory at any and every hazard.

Resolved, unanimously, That the governor be requested to transmit a copy of this report to the governors of each of the States of this Union, and to our senators and representatives in the Congress of the United States.

In the House of Representatives,
December 12, 1848.

Resolved, That the House do agree to the report unanimously.
Ordered, That it be sent to the Senate for concurrence.
By order:

T. W. GLOVER, *C. H. R.*

In the Senate, *December* 15, 1848.

Resolved, That the Senate do unanimously concur in the report.

EXTINCTION OF SLAVERY.

RESOLUTIONS

OF THE

LEGISLATURE OF NEW HAMPSHIRE,

RELATIVE TO

Slavery in the District of Columbia and territories belonging or which may hereafter belong to the United States.

December 29, 1846.
Read, and laid upon the table.

STATE OF NEW HAMPSHIRE.

Resolved by the Senate and House of Representatives in General Court convened, That the Senators and Representatives from this State in the Congress of the United States be respectively requested to urge in that body the passage of measures providing for the extinction of slavery in the District of Columbia; for its exclusion from Oregon, and other Territories that now or at any time hereafter may belong to the United States; for all constitutional measures for the suppression of the domestic slave-trade; and to resist the admission of any new State into the Union while tolerating slavery.

Resolved, That his excellency the governor be requested to furnish copies of the foregoing resolution to the legislatures of the several States, and to our Senators and Representatives in Congress.

JOHN P. HALE,
Speaker of the House of Representatives.

JAMES U. PARKER,
President of the Senate.

Approved July 10, 1846.

ANTHONY COLBY, *Governor.*

A true copy:

GEORGE G. FOGG,
Secretary of State.

BLACK CONSCIOUSNESS: EARLY ORGANIZATION, PROTEST AND DIRECT ACTION

The eminent scholar Benjamin Quarles, has written:

> *"The important role of the Negro in the crusades on his own behalf has generally been overlooked by historians. White Southerners vigorously attacked the abolition movement as a matter of course, but they had to ignore the blacks taking part in it. Many of them were runaway slaves and to acknowledge their existence would have been to undercut the Southerners' own position that the docile and apathetic sons of Africa were well-adapted, loyal slaves. White abolitionists, too, knew something of the role played by black men and women. But, hostile though they were to slavery, these reformers could not bring themselves to regard the Negro as an equal or his role in the movement as a major one. Rather, they tended to view their black coworkers as little more than extras in their own performance, spear carriers in the background without faces."* *

Dr. Quarles' assessment is especially applicable to the period beginning in the 1830's when third party politicians and workingmen's groups initiated the convention movement. Like all other serious leaders, blacks recognized the need to organize or perish and Bishop Richard Allen of the African Methodist Episcopal Church, called the spokesmen together in Philadelphia in 1830, and launched a protest movement which spread throughout the northeast.

The leadership cadre, generally artisans who were self-educated, met to analyze the causes of their disadvantaged status and devise means to effect elevation and improvement. So keenly aware were they of the crucial nature of their responsibility that they made sure they left publications of the entire proceedings for future generations.

The Rochester Convention in 1853 issued a call signed by such stalwarts as James McCune Smith, J.W.C. Pennington, John Mercer Langston, Frederick Douglass, and J.W. Loguen, declaring: "Under the whole heavens, there is not to be found a people which can show better cause for assembling in such a Convention than we."

*Benjamin Quarles, "Freedom's Black Vanguard", Key Issues in the Afro-American Experience, ed. by Nathin Huggins, et. al., (New York, 1971), Vol. I, page 174.

Rochester Convention — The Address of the Colored National Convention to The People of the United States contained the following passages:

> *"We are Americans, and as Americans, we would speak to Americans. We address you not as aliens nor as exiles, humbly asking to be permitted to dwell among you in peace; but we address you as American citizens asserting their rights on their own native soil . . . In assembling ourselves together as we have done, our object is not to excite pity for ourselves, but to command respect for our cause, and to obtain justice for our people."*

Blacks were active in state, national and international conventions during the heat of the anti-slavery campaign, for they were cognizant of their ability to exert significant influence in the political arena even after they had been defranchised in most places. When the demise of slavery appeared certain leaders moved their fight for suffrage into high gear, declaring in the Syracuse, 1864, meeting: "We want the elective franchise in all the States now in the Union and the same in all such states as may come into the Union hereafter."

The Syracuse Convention also drew up the Preamble and Constitution for the establishment of the National Equal Rights League. In addition, they passed and proclaimed a Bill of Wrongs and Rights, stating: "We claim the right to be heard in the halls of Congress; and we claim our fair share of the public domain; whether acquired by purchase, treaty, confiscation or military conquest."

Justifying their demand for full citizenship, convention officers asserted:

> *"Whatever prejudice and taste may be innocently allowed to do or to dictate in social and domestic relations, it is plain that in the matter of government, the object of which is the protection and security of human rights, prejudice should be allowed no voice whatever. In this department of human relations, no notice should be taken of the color of men; but justice, wisdom and humanity should weigh alone and be all-controlling."*

Complete copies of the proceedings of the conventions referred to in this publication are available in the Reserve Room of the Allegheny Campus Library. They were copied from P.V. 409 Rare Books Section of the Pennsylvania State Library, Department of Education in Harrisburg, PA.

Before General Robert E. Lee surrendered at Appomattox in April, 1865, black men all over the nation were mapping strategies to mount campaigns for equal rights. Pennsylvanians met in Harrisburg in February, 1865 to inform the Commonwealth that they were not willing to accept less than first class citizenship. Having noted that more than 8,000 blacks from the Keystone state fought in the Union army, they declared:

> *"We believe that no people have greater reason to complain, or have suffered greater and more frequent cruelties and injustices, or received less consideration for long and faithful services in promoting the general interests of the State, or have been more patient, law-abiding and discreet, than have been the colored people of the State of Pennsylvania."*

Despite the best efforts of the Civil War generation, Pennsylvania delayed the passage of an equal rights law until 1935 when Gov. George Earle signed Act No. 132 following a long hard fight spearheaded by the NAACP.

Champions of white supremacy held mass meetings "to oppose Negro equality" immediately after the passage of the Thirteenth Constitutional amendment in 1865 banning slavery. The broadside "Democratic Meeting" shown in this section was circulated during the congressional elections, urging the people of Kirksville in Adair County, Missouri, to join the fight.

PROCEEDINGS OF THE
NATIONAL CONVENTION,

HELD IN ROCHESTER ON THE 6TH, 7TH AND 8TH OF JULY, 1853.

FIRST DAY—MORNING SESSION.

Pursuant to the Call, the Convention assembled in Corinthian Hall on Wednesday, July 6th, 1853, and was called to order by Rev. Amos G. Beman of Connecticut.

On motion of Rev. Charles B. Ray, of New York, the Rev. John Peck, of Pittsburgh, Pa., was appointed President pro tem.; and Wm. Whipper, of Pennsylvania, and Wm. C. Nell, of Massachusetts, were appointed Secretaries pro tem. James McCune Smith, M. D., then read the Call for the Convention.

On motion of David Jenkings, of Ohio, the delegates were called upon by States, to present their credentials.

Moved by James McCune Smith, that the signers of the Call be considered members *de facto* of this body, whether elected or not. After some discussion, on motion of Wm. H. Day, it was amended so as to read that the signers to the Call of this Convention be, and are hereby constituted members of this Convention. The amendment was carried, and the motions as amended was then adopted.

It was moved that a Committee of eight be appointed by the Chair to nominate officers for the convention. The Chair appointed the following, named persons said Committee: James McCune Smith, Rev. L. A. Grimes, Rev. Stephen Smith, Wm. H. Day, T. G. Campbell, Rev. Byrd Parker, Rev. A. G. Beman, Rev. Wm. C. Munroe.

On motion, the Convention adjourned to meet at 2½ P. M.

AFTERNOON SESSION.

Convention met at 2½ P. M. Rev. John Peck, President, pro tem., in the Chair. Prayer by Rev. Jehial C. Beman. The Committee on nominations reported by their Chairman, James McCune Smith, the following named persons as officers of this Convention:

President—James W. C. Pennington, D. D., of New York; *Vice President*—Wm. H. Day, of Ohio; Amos G. Beman, Connecticut; Wm. C. Nell, Massachusetts; Frederick Douglass, New York; James C. McCrumbell, and John B. Vashon, Pennsylvania; John Jones, Illinois.

Secretaries—Peter H. Clarke, Ohio; Chas. B. Ray and Wm. J. Wilson, New York; Charles L. Reason, Pennsylvania.

The President, on taking the Chair, made a short address. The officers were invited to their respective seats.

BLACK LEADERS UNDERSTOOD THE NEED FOR POLITICAL POWER

Even before the war to end slavery was over black leaders understood the urgency of securing voting rights to give meaning to their status as free citizens.

PROCEEDINGS

OF THE

National Convention of Colored Men,

HELD IN

THE CITY OF SYRACUSE, N. Y.,

OCTOBER 4, 5, 6, AND 7, 1864;

WITH THE

BILL OF WRONGS AND RIGHTS,

AND THE

ADDRESS TO THE AMERICAN PEOPLE.

PRINTED FOR AND BY ORDER OF THE CONVENTION.

1864.

PITTSBURGH BLACK PIONEERS LEFT COMPLETE RECORD OF FIRST POLITICAL CONVENTION

PROCEEDINGS

OF THE

STATE CONVENTION

OF THE

COLORED FREEMEN OF PENNSYLVANIA,

HELD IN PITTSBURGH,

ON THE 23D, 24TH AND 25TH OF AUGUST, 1841,

FOR THE PURPOSE OF

CONSIDERING THEIR CONDITION,

AND

THE MEANS OF ITS IMPROVEMENT

PITTSBURGH

PRINTED BY MATTHEW M. GRANT.

1841.

Pittsburgh leaders called the first statewide black political convention in 1841. Among the committee members who issued the official call were Martin R. Delany, John Templeton, and Lewis Woodson.

SPEECH OF GERRIT SMITH

In the Pittsburg Convention, August 12th, 1852.

(WRITTEN OUT BY HIMSELF.)

For a long time, I have been able to entertain but little hope, that this superlatively guilty nation can be saved. Indeed, its salvation seems to be well nigh impossible.

Perhaps, there are other nations, that are committing as great crimes against humanity, as this nation is.—but they are not, like this nation, committing them in the name both of republicanism and christianity. If the condition of this nation is hopeless, it is hopeless for no other reason so much, as for the reason, that it is the republican form of politics and the christian form of religion, which she has prostituted to the purposes of oppression. Were the structure of her government despotic, and were her system of religion heathen, there might be hope of regenerating and saving the nation, by republicanizing her politics and christianizing her religion. But, now, that she has turned into darkness the greatest of all political lights and the greatest of all religious lights, what hope is left for her? If these unequalled lights, which were in her, have become darkness, how great is that darkness! If she has succeeded in corrupting, perverting, and making void both republicanism and christianity, what agency can be found mighty enough to control and restore her? Nevertheless, I will not, utterly, despair of my country:—and, surely, it is not for me to set limits to the mercy and power of God.

I came to this Convention with but little hope, that this pre-eminently guilty nation can be saved. I shall return from it with, probably, as little—perhaps with less. I say so, for the reason, that I do not expect, that this Convention will take such action, as, I believe, it must take, in order, that it may exert a saving influence upon the nation. Nevertheless, there is an action, which, were this Convention to take it, would send me home hopeful and rejoicing. Oh yes, there is an action, which, were this Convention to take it, would ray with hope the clouds, which shut in so close and so black around our country. But, why have I referred to this action? You will not take it. You are not yet, prepared to take it. And when, at last, you shall be prepared to take it;—and when, at last, you shall see the indispensableness of it;—then, in all probability, it will be too late;—for, then, in all probability, our country, if not already ruined, will be ruined—irretrievably ruined.

I have, for some half dozen years, been beseeching the virtuous voters of the country to take such action, as I would, now, commend to you, had I any encouragement to commend it to you. But, in all these beseechings, during all this time, I have seemed to them, as one, that mocked.

I said, that I would commend this action to you, had I any encouragement to do so. But, is it, even, worth while for me to tell you what this action is? [Yes! yes! tell it! tell it!] You will, then, bear with me, in telling it, will you? [We will! we will!]

Well, the action, which I wish you to take, consists of but two things. The first is to organize yourselves into a party, which shall be as comprehensive, in its scope and purpose, as is civil government itself: and the second is to make honesty, or, in other words, the doing unto others, as you would have others do unto you, the ruling principle of such organization.

But, in organizing yourself into such a party, you will imply, that you have left the great political parties forever. And you, surely, are not yet prepared, are you? to say, that you have left them *forever?* [We are! we are?] But, are you not calculating to return to them, at some future period? [No! no!] Indeed! Is it so? Well, I had supposed, that you were not yet entirely weaned from those flesh-pots of Egypt. I had supposed, that, unlike the men of strong faith, of whom Paul speaks, you were still mindful of that country, from whence you had come out. I had supposed, that you were not yet brought to the settled and unalterable conclusion, that these great parties have passed the bounds and the possibility of reformation; and are, now, not only, *utterly* abominable, but *incorrigibly* abominable. I had supposed, that you still believe, that these parties are capable of regeneration and future usefulness, notwithstanding, that, in this noon of the nineteenth century, they can pledge themselves to uphold slavery and the diabolical fugitive slave law, and to "discountenance", and "resist", the discussion of these subjects.

Pious Lot left Sodom, not with the purpose of returning to it, after it should be reformed. He left it, because he believed, that it was no longer capable of being reformed. He left it, because he believed, that it was to be destroyed. Thus, should men leave the Whig and Democratic parties—those Modern Sodoms—not expecting ever to return to them; but flying from them, as from a determined and certain destruction. And, as they fly, they should cast no wishful looks behind. Remember Lot's wife. They should stay not in all the plain of vulgar, corrupt, satanic politics. But, lest they, also, be consumed, they should hasten to the mountain of righteous politics.

Gerrit Smith Circular, Moorland-Spingarn Collection, Howard University, Washington, D.C.

For further information on the 1852 meeting, see **American Reformers**, ed. Carlos Martyn, New York, Funk & Wagnalls, 1891, p. 210, 213.

On August 11, 1852, the Free Soil Party Convention met in Pittsburgh. Rochester, New York sent a black delegate, Frederick Douglass, who was made secretary. Gerrit Smith voiced his deep concern for the "great crimes against humanity".

PROCEEDINGS OF

THE STATE EQUAL RIGHTS' CONVENTION OF THE COLORED MEN OF PENNSYLVANIA,

HELD IN THE CITY OF HARRISBURG,

FEBRUARY 8TH, 9TH, AND 10TH, 1865.

In accordance with a call issued by the Pennsylvania State Equal Rights' League, the Convention was convened in the Union Wesleyan Church, Harrisburg, on Wednesday morning, February 8th, at 10 o'clock.

Mr. William Nesbitt of Altoona, Vice President of the State League, called the Convention to order, and by common consent, acted as its temporary Chairman, and Mr. Octavius V. Catto, of Philadelphia, as Secretary.

By invitation of the Chairman, the Rev. John Price of Harrisburg, offered a prayer for the guidance and blessing of God during the deliberations of the Convention.

On motion of Mr. C. H. Vance, the Convention appointed the following gentlemen a Committee on Credentials:—

CHARLES H. VANCE, *of Harrisburg*,
O. L. C. HUGHES, *of Harrisburg*,
MOSES BROWN, *of Hollidaysburg*,
WILLIAM COOPER, *of Philadelphia*,
JAMES DAVENGER, *of Pittston*.

The first six seats across the front of the Church, were, on motion of Mr. A. M. Green, set apart for the accommodation of the members of the Convention.

The State Equal Rights' Convention of The Colored Men of Pennsylvania P.V. 409, Pennsylvania State Library, Harrisburg, PA

FARMER AN[D] WHO PAY TAXES

GREENBACK ARE GOOD ENOUGH FOR THE MECHANIC

THEY ARE GOOD ENOUGH FOR THE BOND HOLDER WHO PAYS NO TAXES

DEMOCRATIC MEETING.

ALL WHO ARE OPPOSED TO

NEGRO EQUALITY!

AND CONGRESSIONAL USURPATIONS,

and in favor of the payment of the

NATIONAL DEBT

IN GREENBACKS,

EQUAL TAXATION, ABROGATION OF THE "TEST OATH" AND SECURING TO ALL THE States of the Union their Rights under the Federal Constitution.

Are cordially invited to be present and take part in the deliberations at a

MASS MEETING,

at Sherwood's hall, February 22, '68.

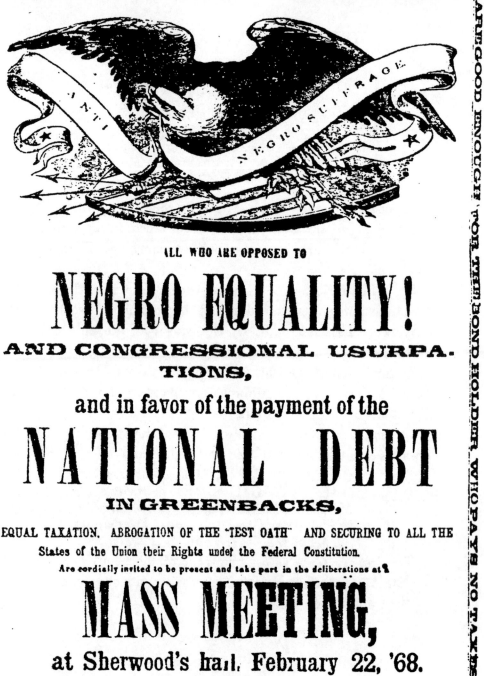

FACSIMILE OF POLITICAL POSTER IN THE CAMPAIGN OF 1868.
The original belongs to F. M. Harrington, Kirksville.

E.M. Violette, History of Adair County, (Denslow History Co. 1911) p. 72. Public Library, Kansas City, Missouri

SOME FREE BLACKS: 1860

Examination of the table on Population by Color and Condition reveals the varying patterns of distribution of the free colored population in six Southern states during 1860. An intriguing picture emerges as we see the marked disparity in the frequency of free status among those persons within the free colored class identified as blacks and mulattoes.

There is a widely-held notion that mulattoes received preferential treatment in both self-purchase and benevolent manumissions because, in many cases, they represented children of master-class fathers and slave mothers. The figures for Alabama, North Carolina, and Louisiana, showing sharply-skewed distribution in the mulatto division might be used to support this hypothesis. However, figures for Virginia and Maryland show the majority of free colored were blacks. The Maryland figure of 67,902 blacks out of a total free colored population of 83,942 appears to indicate prejudice in favor of black skin. In Mississippi, with a very small free colored population, rather evenly divided, it seems pigmentation meant very little.

This illustration strongly suggests that no hard and fast rules can be established to cover the endless continuum of human relationships which existed within the system of slavery. It can also be inferred that no two combinations of whites and blacks exhibited the same behavioral patterns toward each other, a consequence of the infinite number of hidden psychological variables impossible to record and subject to cold scientific diagnosis.

1860 POPULATION BY COLOR AND CONDITION

STATE	WHITE	FREE COLORED		SLAVES	AGGREGATE
		Blacks	Mulattoes		
Alabama	526,431	592	2,098	435,000	964,201
North Carolina	631,000	8,655	21,808	331,059	992,622
Virginia	1,047,411	34,557	23,485	490,865	1,596,318
Louisiana	357,629	3,489	15,158	331,726	708,002
Maryland	515,918	67,902	16,040	87,189	687,049
Mississippi	353,901	372	401	436,631	971,305

The figures above were compiled from Table 3 of the 1860 Census, (Eighth Census), Government Printing Office, Washington, D.C., 1864. Data were copied from the following pages: Alabama, 8; North Carolina, 359; Virginia, 518; Louisiana, 194; Maryland, 214; Mississippi, 270.

THE CIVIL WAR AND EMANCIPATION

Frederick Douglass, the great orator, was joined in a call to arms by leaders of the black communities everywhere. These men, many of whom had been active in the convention movements and the anti-slavery campaigns, demonstrated their willingness to pay whatever price was demanded for freedom and dignity. They proclaimed:

> *"For generations we have suffered under the horrors of slavery, outrage and wrong; our manhood has been denied, our citizenship blotted out, our souls seared and burned, our spirits cowed and crushed, and the hopes of the future of our race involved in doubts and darkness. But now the whole aspect of our relations to the white race is changed. Now, therefore, is our most precious moment. Let us Rush to Arms! Fail now and our race is doomed on this the soil of our birth. We must now awake, arise or be forever fallen."*

Not only black Americans but numerous white men were willing to fight for more than union – they demanded freedom and justice for all. John Brown, the hero of Harper's Ferry, disturbed the conscience of a nation in his willingness to die for the freedom of his black brother.

Charles Sumner was one of those Radical Republicans who led the congressional fight against slave power. He reminded Americans that all their ancestors shared the common experience of slavery. Whites were being sold in North Africa during the late eighteenth century when Americans fought the Barbary States and the national government paid large sums for the ransom of many United States citizens.

Four days after Emancipation Proclamation, Jefferson Davis, the Confederate President, issued his decree dooming all free blacks to perpetual slavery, declaring that black servitude was the "cornerstone" of the Southern Confederacy. Fortunately, the greater coercive power of the Union thwarted his intent.

Thomas Wentworth Higginson, a sensitive white officer who commanded the black First South Carolina Volunteers, asked the crucial question:

> *"Is there no limit, no end to the injustice we heap upon this unfortunate people? Cannot even the fact of their being in arms for the nation, liable to die any day in its defense, secure them ordinary justice?"*

· THE GREAT CIVIL WAR ·

. . . THE ENROLLMENT IN THE UNITED STATES ARMY . . .

The following table shows the total number of men furnished by each of the several States for the United States army during the Civil War of 1861-1865. The first column of figures shows the number furnished under the call of President Lincoln for 75,000 troops, issued April 15, 1861. The second column shows the aggregate number of white men furnished under all the calls:

STATES.	First Call.	All Calls.
Maine	771	71,715
New Hampshire	779	34,605
Vermont	782	35,246
Massachusetts	3,736	151,785
Rhode Island	3,147	23,711
Connecticut	2,402	57,270
New York	13,906	464,156
New Jersey	3,123	79,511
Pennsylvania	20,175	366,326
Delaware	775	13,651
Maryland	......	49,731
West Virginia	900	32,003
District of Columbia	4,720	16,872
Ohio	12,557	317,133
Indiana	4,686	195,147
Illinois	4,820	258,217
Michigan	781	90,119
Wisconsin	817	96,118
Minnesota	930	25,034
Iowa	968	75,860
Missouri	10,501	108,773
Kentucky	......	78,540
Kansas	650	20,097
Tennessee	......	12,077
Arkansas	......	....
North Carolina	......	....
California	......	7,451
Nevada	......	216
Oregon	......	617
Washington	......	895
Nebraska	......	1,279
Colorado	......	1,762
Dakota	......	181
New Mexico	1,510	2,395
TOTAL	93,326	2,688,523

The following exhibit gives the number of colored and drafted troops furnished to the Union army by the different States including the States which were in rebellion; besides which 92,576 colored troops were included (with the white soldiers) in the quotas of the several States. Many who enlisted from the South were credited to Northern States:

STATES AND TERRITORIES.	Colored Troops. 1861-65.	Number Drafted.	Bounties Paid by States.
NEW ENGLAND STATES.			
Connecticut	1,764	12,031	$ 6,887,554
Maine	104	27,324	7,837,644
Massachusetts	3,966	41,582	22,965,550
New Hampshire	125	10,806	9,636,313
Rhode Island	1,837	4,321	820,769
Vermont	120	7,743	4,528,775
TOTAL	7,916	103,807	52,676,605
MIDDLE STATES.			
New Jersey	1,185	32,325	23,868,967
New York	4,125	151,488	86,629,228
Pennsylvania	8,612	178,873	43,154,987
TOTAL	13,922	362,686	153,653,182
WESTERN STATES AND TERRITORIES.			
Colorado Territory	95	......	....
Illinois	1,811	32,085	17,296,205
Indiana	1,537	41,158	9,182,354
Iowa	440	7,548	1,615,171
Kansas	2,080	1,420	57,407
Michigan	1,387	22,022	9,664,855
Minnesota	104	10,796	2,000,464
Ohio	5,092	50,400	23,557,878
Wisconsin	165	38,395	5,855,356
TOTAL	12,711	203,924	69,229,185
BORDER STATES.			
Delaware	954	8,635	1,136,599
District of Columbia	3,269	14,338	184,010
Kentucky	23,703	29,421	692,577
Maryland	8,718	29,319	6,271,992
Missouri	8,344	21,519	1,282,149
West Virginia	196	3,180	864,737
TOTAL	45,184	106,412	10,882,064
SOUTHERN STATES.			
Alabama	4,969	......	....
Arkansas	5,526	......	....
Florida	1,044	......	....
Georgia	......	......	....
Louisiana	3,486	......	....
Mississippi	17,869	......	....
North Carolina	5,035	......	....
South Carolina	5,462	......	....
Tennessee	20,133	......	....
Texas	47	......	....
Virginia	......	......	....
TOTAL	63,571	......	....
GRAND TOTAL	173,079	776,829	$285,941,030
At large	733	......	....
Not accounted for	5,083	......	....
Officers	7,122	......	....
TOTAL	186,017	......	....

ACTIVISTS FROM EVERY WALK OF LIFE JOINED DOUGLASS IN MOBILIZATION OF BLACK TROOPS TO FIGHT FOR THE UNION CAUSE.

MEN OF COLOR, TO ARMS! NOW OR NEVER!

This is our Golden Moment. The Government of the United States calls for every Able-Bodied Colored Man to enter the Army for the **THREE YEARS' SERVICE**, and join in fighting the Battles of Liberty and the Union. A new era is open to us. For generations we have suffered under the horrors of slavery, outrage and wrong; our manhood has been denied, our citizenship blotted out, our souls seared and burned, our spirits cowed and crushed, and the hopes of the future of our race involved in doubts and darkness. But now the whole aspect of our relations to the white race is changed. Now therefore is our most precious moment. Let us Rush to Arms! **Fail Now and Our Race is Doomed** on this the soil of our birth. We must now awake, arise, or be forever fallen. If we value Liberty, if we wish to be free in this land, if we love our country, if we love our families, our children, our homes, we must strike NOW while the Country calls: must rise up in the dignity of our manhood, and show by our own right arms that we are worthy to be freemen. Our enemies have made the country believe that we are craven cowards, without soul, without manhood, without the spirit of soldiers. Shall we die with this stigma resting on our graves? Shall we leave this inheritance of shame to our children? No! A thousand times No! **We WILL Rise!** The alternative is upon us; let us rather die freemen than live to be slaves. What is life without liberty? We say that we have manhood—now is the time to prove it. A nation or a people that cannot fight may be pitied, but cannot be respected. If we would be regarded *Men*, if we would forever **SILENCE THE TONGUE OF CALUMNY,** of prejudice and hate; let us rise NOW and fly to arms! We have seen what **Valor and Heroism** our brothers displayed at **PORT HUDSON and at MILLIKEN'S BEND;** though they are just from the galling, poisoning grasp of slavery, they have startled the world by the most exalted heroism. If they have proved themselves heroes, can not we prove ourselves men? **ARE FREEMEN LESS BRAVE THAN SLAVES?** More than a Million White Men have left Comfortable Homes and joined the Armies of the Union to save their Country; cannot we leave ours, and swell the hosts of the Union, to save our liberties, vindicate our manhood, and deserve well of our Country?

MEN OF COLOR! All Races of Men—the Englishman, the Irishman, the Frenchman, the German, the American, have been called to assert their claim to freedom and a manly character, by an appeal to the sword. The day that has seen an enslaved race in arms, has, in all history, seen their last trial. We can now see that **OUR LAST OPPORTUNITY HAS COME!** If we are not lower in the scale of humanity than Englishmen, Irishmen, white Americans and other races, we can show it now.

MEN OF COLOR! BROTHERS and FATHERS! WE APPEAL TO YOU! By all your concern for yourselves and your liberties, by all your regard for God and Humanity, by all your desire for Citizenship and Equality before the law, by all your love for the Country, to stop at no subterfuges, listen to nothing that shall deter you from rallying for the Army. Come forward, and at once Enroll your Names for the **Three Years' Service. STRIKE NOW,** and you are henceforth and forever **FREEMEN!**

E. D. Bassett,
Wm. D. Forten,
Frederick Douglass,
Wm. Whipper,
D. D. Turner,
Jas. McCrummell,
A. S. Cassey,
A. M. Green,
J. W. Page,
L. R. Seymour,
Rev. J. Underdue,
John W. Price,
Augustus Dorsey,
Rev. Stephen Smith,
N. W. Depee,
Dr. J. H. Wilson,
J. W. Cassey,
P. J. Armstrong,
J. W. Simpson,
Rev. J B Trusty,
S. Morgan Smith,
Wm. E. Gipson,
Rev. J. Boulden,
Rev. J. Asher,
Rev. J. C. Gibbs,
Daniel George,
Robert M. Adger,
Henry M. Cropper,
Rev. J. B. Reeve,
Rev. J. A. Williams,
Rev. A. L. Stanford,
Thomas J. Bowers,
Elijah J. Davis,
John P. Burr,
Robert Jones,
O. V. Catto,
Thos. J. Dorsey,
I. D. Cliff,
Jacob C. White,
Morris Hall,
James Needham,
Rev. Elisha Weaver,
Ebenezer Black,
Rev. Wm. T. Catto,
Jas. R. Gordon,
Samuel Stewart,
David B. Bowser,
Henry Minton,
Daniel Colley,
J. C. White, Jr.,
Rev. J. P. Campbell,
Rev. W. J. Alston,
J. P. Johnson,
Franklin Turner,
Jesse E. Glasgow.

THE HONORED MARTYR OF HARPER'S FERRY

John Brown and his family were willing to die for the cause of freedom.

From the private collection of David Henley, Pittsburgh, PA

Whites as well as blacks felt the "galling yoke of slavery" during the colonial and pre-Civil War period. The following page ad was published in A Key to Uncle Tom's Cabin by Harriet Beecher Stowe, Boston: 1853. Note reference to book on white slavery by famous senator, Charles Sumner.

NEW BOOKS,

OF RARE INTEREST AND VALUE,

JUST PUBLISHED BY

JOHN P. JEWETT AND COMPANY,

BOSTON.

Owing to the unparalleled draft upon our resources, during the past year, on account of the unexampled sale of UNCLE TOM'S CABIN, a large number of most valuable manuscripts were obliged to lie untouched in our safe, waiting a favorable moment to appear in print. We have availed ourselves of the earliest moment, and now offer them to the *readers of good books*. Most of them are issued. Those still in press will be published speedily.

THE SHADY SIDE;

OR, LIFE IN A COUNTRY PARSONAGE.

BY A PASTOR'S WIFE.

This volume is designed, in a measure, as a contrast to that charming little book, *Sunny Side*, and we doubt not that it will meet with quite as favorable a reception as that work. It is written in an admirable style, and he who commences its perusal will hardly be able to stop until he has gone through. Price 75 cents.

COUNT STRUENZEE, THE SCEPTIC AND THE CHRISTIAN.

TRANSLATED FROM THE GERMAN BY MRS. WILSON.

This most interesting work contains the history of the last days of this distinguished man, and the account of his numerous interviews and conversations with his pastor, Munter, through whose instrumentality he was led to abandon his scepticism, and embrace the religion of Jesus. Price 62½ cents.

THE LAST HOURS OF CHRIST.

BY W. G. SCHAUFFLER, MISSIONARY AT CONSTANTINOPLE.

A portion of this most admirably written volume of Meditations on the last hours of our Saviour upon earth was published some years since, and met with great favor from the religious public. The work has been re-written, and very much enlarged, and is again offered to the community. We would not say a word in its commendation to those who have read the volume as originally published. To those who love to go with the Redeemer of men, to meditate in the garden of Gethsemane, or upon the Mount of Olives, or by the Sea of Galilee, this volume will afford a vein of sacred thought. Price $1.

DR. BEECHER'S THIRD VOLUME.

We have just issued the third volume in the series of the writings of this venerable and eloquent man, as has been lately said of him by some one, "*the father of more brains than any other man in the country.*" This volume contains his VIEWS OF THEOLOGY, and his celebrated Trial for Heresy before the Presbytery and Synod of Cincinnati. With a *superb steel Portrait*, by Andrews. Price $1. *No clergyman's library is complete* without Dr. Beecher's writings.

WHITE SLAVERY IN THE BARBARY STATES.

BY HON. CHARLES SUMNER, U. S. S.

ILLUSTRATED BY 40 SUPERB DESIGNS BY BILLINGS, ENGRAVED BY BAKER, SMITH AND ANDREWS

This superb volume in its typography and illustrations, and elegant in its composition, being one of the finest productions of its accomplished author, is offered to the public in this most attractive form, with the hope that thousands may peruse its glowing pages, and from them receive fresh stimulus in their efforts to elevate humanity from degradation and wrong. They will learn from it that in years past *white men* as well as blacks have felt the galling yoke of slavery. Price 50 cents.

JUDGE JAY'S WRITINGS ON SLAVERY.

In one volume, 12mo, with a Portrait. Price $1.

Who has rendered more efficient services to the cause of humanity than the venerable Judge Jay? His collective writings will be among the very best contributions to the anti-slavery literature of the country.

AN ADDRESS TO THE PEOPLE OF THE FREE STATES

BY THE

PRESIDENT OF THE SOUTHERN CONFEDERACY.

RICHMOND, January 5, 1863.

Citizens of the non-slave-holding States of America, swayed by peaceable motives, I have used all my influence, often thereby endangering my position as the President of the Southern Confederacy, to have the unhappy conflict now existing between my people and yourselves, governed by those well established international rules, which heretofore have softened the asperities which necessarily are the concomitants of a state of belligerency, but all my efforts in the premises have heretofore been unavailing. Now, therefore, I am compelled *e necessitati rei* to employ a measure, which most willingly I would have omitted to do, regarding, as I always must, State Rights, as the very organism of politically associated society.

For nearly two years my people have been defending their inherent rights—their political, social and religious rights against the speculators of New England and their allies in the States heretofore regarded as conservative. The people of the Southern Confederacy have—making sacrifices such as the modern world has never witnessed—patiently, but determinedly, stood between their home interests and the well paid, well fed and well clad mercenaries of the Abolitionists, and I need not say that they have nobly vindicated the good name of American citizens. Heretofore, the warfare has been conducted by white men—peers, scions of the same stock; but the programme has been changed, and your rulers despairing of a triumph by the employment of white men, have degraded you and themselves, by inviting the co-operation of the black race. Thus, while they deprecate the intervention of white men—the French and the English—in behalf of the Southern Confederacy, they, these Abolitionists, do not hesitate to invoke the intervention of the African race in favor of the North.

The time has, therefore, come when a becoming respect for the good opinion of the civilized world impels me to set forth the following facts:—

First. Abraham Lincoln,, the President of the Non-Slaveholding States, has issued his proclamation, declaring the slaves within the limits of the Southern Confederacy to be free.

Second. Abraham Lincoln has declared that the slaves so emancipated may be used in the Army and Navy, now under his control, by which he means to employ, against the Free People of the South, insurrectionary measures, the inevitable tendency of which will be to inaugurate a Servile War, and thereby prove destructive, in a great measure, to slave property.

Now, therefore, as a compensatory measure, I do hereby issue the following Address to the People of the Non-Slaveholding States:—

On and after February 22, 1863, all free negroes within the limits of the Southern Confederacy shall be placed on the slave status, and be deemed to be chattels, they and their issue forever.

All negroes who shall be taken in any of the States in which Slavery does not now exist, in the progress of our arms, shall be adjudged, immediately after such capture, to occupy the slave status, and in all States which shall be vanquished by our arms, all free negroes shall, *ipso facto*, be reduced to the condition of helotism, so that the respective normal conditions of the white and black races may be ultimately placed on a permanent basis, so as to prevent the public peace from being thereafter endangered.

Therefore, while I would not ignore the conservative policy of the Slave States, namely, that a Federal Government cannot, without violating the fundamental principles of a Constitution, interfere with the internal policy of several States; since, however, Abraham Lincoln has seen fit to ignore the Constitution he has solemnly sworn to support, it ought not to be considered polemically or politically improper in me to vindicate the position which has been, at an early day of this Southern republic, assumed by the Confederacy, namely, that slavery is the corner-stone of a Western Republic. It is not necessary for me to elaborate this proposition. I may merely refer, in passing, to the prominent fact, that the South is emphatically a producing section of North America; this is equally true of the West and Northwest, the people of which have been mainly dependent on the South for the consumption of their products. The other States, in which slavery does not exist, have occupied a middle position, as to the South, West and Northwest. The States of New England, from which all complicated difficulties have arisen, owe their greatness and power to the free suffrages of all other sections of North America; and yet, as is now evident, they have, from the adoption of the Federal Constitution, waged a persistent warfare against the interests of all the other States of the old Union. The great centre of their opposition has been Slavery, while the annual statistics of their respective State Governments abundantly prove that they entertain within all their boundaries fewer negroes than any single State which does not tolerate slavery.

In view of these facts, and conscientiously believing that the proper condition of the negro is slavery, or a complete subjection to the white man,—and entertaining the belief that the day is not distant when the old Union will be restored with slavery nationally declared to be the proper condition of all of African descent,—and in view of the future harmony and progress of all the States of America, I have been induced to issue this address, so that there may be no misunderstanding in the future.

JEFFERSON DAVIS.

Richmond Enquirer Print.

Slavery Papers, Henry P. Slaughter Collection, Trevor Arnett Library, Atlanta University, Atlanta, GA.

fix upon the North a brand of meanness worse than either Southerner or Englishman has yet dared to impute. The mere delay in the fulfilment of this contract has already inflicted untold suffering, has impaired discipline, has relaxed loyalty, and has begun to implant a feeling of sullen distrust in the very regiments whose early career solved the problem of the nation, created a new army, and made peaceful emancipation possible.

T. W. HIGGINSON,
Colonel commanding **1st S. C. Vols.**

BEAUFORT, S. C., January 22, 1864.

HEADQUARTERS FIRST SOUTH CAROLINA VOLUNTEERS,
BEAUFORT, S. C., Sunday, February 14, 1864.

To the Editor of the New York Times:

May I venture to call your attention to the great and cruel injustice which is impending over the brave men of this regiment?

They have been in military service for over a year, having volunteered, every man, without a cent of bounty, on the written pledge of the War Department that they should receive the same pay and rations with white soldiers.

This pledge is contained in the written instructions of Brigadier-General Saxton, Military Governor, dated August 25, 1862. Mr. Solicitor Whiting, having examined those instructions, admits to me that "the faith of the Government was thereby pledged to every officer and soldier under that call."

Surely, if this fact were understood, every man in the nation would see that the Government is degraded by using for a year the services of the brave soldiers, and then repudiating the contract under which they were enlisted. This is what will be done, should Mr. Wilson's bill, legalizing the back pay of the army, be defeated.

We presume too much on the supposed ignorance of these men. I have never yet found a man in my regiment so stupid as not to know when he was cheated. If fraud proceeds from Government itself, so much the worse, for this strikes at the foundation of all rectitude, all honor, all obligation.

Mr. Senator Fessenden said, in the debate on Mr. Wilson's bill, January 4, that the Government was not bound by the unauthorized promises of irresponsible recruiting officers. But is the Government itself an irresponsible recruiting officer? and if men have volunteered in good faith on the written assurances of the Secretary of War, is not Congress bound, in all decency, either to fulfil those pledges or to disband the regiments?

Mr. Senator Doolittle argued in the same debate that white soldiers should receive higher pay than black ones, because the families of the latter were often supported by Government. What an astounding statement of fact is this! In the white regiment in which I was formerly an officer (the Massachusetts Fifty-First) nine tenths of the soldiers' families, in addition to the pay and bounties, drew regularly their "State aid." Among my black soldiers, with half-pay and no bounty, not a family receives any aid. Is there to be no limit, no end to the injustice we heap upon this unfortunate people? Cannot even the fact of their being in arms for the nation, liable to die any day in its defence, secure them ordinary justice? Is the nation so poor, and so utterly demoralized by its pauperism, that after it has had the lives of these men, it must turn round to filch six dollars of the monthly pay which the Secretary of War promised to their widows? It is even so, if the excuses of Mr. Fessenden and Mr. Doolittle are to be accepted by Congress and by the people.

Very respectfully, your obedient servant,

T. W. HIGGINSON,

Colonel commanding 1st *S. C. Volunteers.*

Higginson, Thomas Wentworth, Army Life in A Black Regiment, Boston: 1870.

THE INDEPENDENT BLACK CHURCH
TOWER OF STRENGTH, FOUNT OF EVERY BLESSING

Any serious discussion of the historical movement of American blacks from slavery to freedom must take into account the crucial role of the independent black Baptist and Methodist churches which emerged during the revolutionary era. Historian Carter G. Woodson notes that the first separate black church was founded in 1773 at Silver Bluff, Georgia and continued to exist until the preacher, David George, and fifty other slaves joined the British in 1778 when they saw a chance to gain their freedom. The Baptist work continued under the leadership of Andrew Bryan, who purchased his freedom in 1789 and in 1790 paid for a lot on which to build Savannah's original meeting house for blacks, the First African Baptist Church. Another pioneer, Rev. Josiah Bishop began his work in Virginia, moved north to Baltimore, and by 1810 was pastor of historic Abyssinia Baptist Church in New York City.

The more forceful agents of social change for blacks, however, were the Methodist clergymen who designed a plan for a strong organizational machine and set in motion a practical vehicle adequate to move forward on the rugged road to spiritual, social, economic, legal, and finally, political opportunity for freedom. The African Methodist Episcopal Church established a national body in 1816 and the African Methodist Episcopal Zion adopted a similar plan in 1822. The AME Church grew rapidly and has continued to expand into the most numerous connectional structure of black communicants in the world including episcopal districts in North America, South America, Europe and Africa.

Looking back over the first fifty years of the existence of the AME Church, in 1867 Bishop Benjamin Tucker Tanner, a native of Pittsburgh, PA, produced a deeply philosophical and an unusually detailed study entitled "Apology for African Methodism". At the outset he explained that the term "apology" was used in the eccelsiastical sense and "not in the sense of an excuse."

Even before Richard Allen and Absolom Jones, unable to bear the burden of hypocritical Christianity, led blacks out of St. George's Methodist Episcopal Church in Philadelphia in 1787, they had formed the Free African Society. They were, in fact, writing their bylaws and forging a permanent union during the same year and in the same neighborhood where the founding fathers of the larger society were writing the United States Constitution. Bishop Tanner extols the virtue of the first sixteen men who met in Philadelphia to pool their resources and establish a network known as the "Bethel Connexion", representing congregations from Pennsylvania, Maryland, Delaware, and New Jersey. Tanner boasted that these were men "who dared to organize a Church of men, men to think for themselves, men to talk for themselves, men to act for themselves: A Church of men who support from their own substance, however scanty, the ministration of the Word which they receive; men who spurn to have their churches built for them, and their pastors supported from the coffers of some charitable organization; men who prefer to live by the sweat of their own brows and be free." *

Paying tribute to Allen for his charismatic leadership, Tanner wrote: "Decision is the stepping-stone to greatness, temporal and eternal; not rashness, not obstinacy, but an enlightened and reasonable decision, that sees a duty, and fears not to perform it. A man of such decided temperament was Richard Allen . . ." **

Richard Allen surveyed the field and concluded that the 100,000 free black people of the northern and border states would accept and spread his "abolition gospel." His followers which included zealots like Morris Brown, Paul Quinn, Daniel Payne and scores of like-minded men preached and taught and worked with such tremendous power that the AME Church grew rapidly and in its golden anniversary year could boast of geographic boundaries coextensive with the nation — Canada included — and fifty thousand paying members and nearly a quarter of a million followers. They had accumulated schools, libraries and one college, Wilberfoce University in Ohio, which they owned and absolutely controlled.

* Benjamin T. Tanner, **An Apology for African Methodism**; Baltimore, 1867, page 16.

**Ibid., page 63.

Gently admonishing those blacks who chose to remain with the larger white controlled Methodist, Presbyterian and Episcopal bodies Tanner poses a series of questions designed to demonstrate the necessity for independent black institutions.

The two charts produced on page fifty compares the first decade with the fifth and illustrates very substantial growth and development.

On page 56, the writer deplores the position of the blacks who remained with the larger Methodist organization noting that they were excluded from policy-making roles and were denied credit for their material contributions. Tanner stated:

> *"The facts obviate the necessity of answering in length, the second portion of the first general interrogatory, to wit: "Would the credit of acquiring these material riches justly redound to the business capacity of the colored race?" We answer in brief. How could it, when white men did all the head-work, when white men really own it, and absolutely control it; a black vote having never been cast, since the church was organized, neither to make a law, nor to annul one."*

Page 57 contains a scathing attack on the Methodist ministers who "thought God too prudent to commission a black Ambassador." He declared "And what was their crime, but acting upon the damnable policy of expediency – of doing what seemed to be necessary, but not just – of compelling the Church, the Church that should account to no man, and to no times, to succumb to the base prejudices of the human heart."

AN APOLOGY

AFRICAN METHODISM,

BY

BENJ. T. TANNER.

BALTIMORE:
1867.

THE SUMMARIES.

OF THE FIRST DECADE.

Circuits		10
Stations		2
Pastors, or Itinerants		17
Salary total in Balto. Dis. for six Pastors	$ 448	30
Bishop's Allowance	25	00
Letter Bill	14	37½
Travelling Expenses	9	00
Sec. " "	9	00
Secretary's Fee	4	00
Livery for Travelling Preachers' horses	8	00
Expenses for Conference Room	3	00
Paid bal. due to Bishop	16	87½
Sum Total	537	55
For Sal. of ten Pastors in Phil. Dis.	604	20½
Total	1151	75½
Our Total Membership		7,937

OF THE FIFTH DECADE.

a. Churches	286	
b. Pastors	185	
c. Annual Conference	10	
d. Circuits	39	
e. Missions	40	
f. Stations	50	
g. S. S. Teachers and School	21,000	
h. Libraries with Vols	17,818	
i. Members of Church	50,000	
j. Aid to Orphans and Widows	$ 5,000	00
k. Support of Pastors.	83,593	00
l. Val. of Church Prop	825,000	00
m. Support of S.	3,000	00
n. Total am't raised	100,000	00

Benevolent Institutions.

a. P. H. and F. Miss. Soc.	1
b. Conf. Miss. Societies	10
c. Preachers' Aid Societies	10
d. Educational Associations	6

Literary Institutions.

a. Literary and Hist. Soc.	5
b. Book Concerns	1
c. Weekly Periodicals	1
d. Collegiate Institutions	1

As we survey these wondrous results, where can fitter words be found than those employed by the Lord's mother.

"My soul doth magnify the Lord. And my spirit hath rejoiced in God my Saviour.

For he hath regarded the low estate of his handmaiden; for behold, from henceforth, all generations shall call me blessed.

For he that is mighty hath done to me great things; and holy is his name.

And his mercy is on them that fear him, from generation to generation.

The answer to Question I, as to material results, is that all the church property in which the colored people worship, who remained in communion with the M. E. Church, together with the publishing houses, the seminaries, the colleges, in short all the material wealth of that princely Connexion, is, with the slightest imaginable fraction, owned exclusively by white people, and exclusively controlled by them: while the hundreds of churches in which those worship, who followed the manly leadership of Allen, are owned exclusively, and controlled exclusively by colored men. This happy result could not possibly have been attained had all the colored Methodists remained with the M. E. Church.

These facts obviate the necessity of answering in length, the second portion of the first general interrogatory, to wit: "Would the credit of acquiring these material riches justly redound to the business capacity of the colored race?" We answer in brief. How could it, when white men did all the headwork, when white men really own it, and absolutely control it; *a black vote having never been cast, since the Church was organized, neither to make a law, nor to annul one.*

The second general interrogatory, will be answered separately, according to the several questions, there propounded.

(*a*) Would as many colored men have been engaged in the Christian Ministry? and have had a field wherein to exercise the "gifts and graces" God had given them?

But why ask this question, when the ruling powers in the M. E. Church, did not believe that God ever called a colored brother to the regular work and honors of the ministry. Be not surprized, good reader, at this apparently rash assertion ; for, be assured, it is said in charity toward the men to whom it relates. These men, christian men withal, gazed upon the condition of affairs — the existence of slavery — the enforcement of the most oppressive laws — the comparative ignorance of the men presenting themselves for the Master's work — the fewness of their brethren to whom they would possibly minister, all these untoward sights appalled them, and made them believe that their colored brother was more likely to be mistaken in his impressions in regard to his call to the ministry, than that the Lord would call him to do a work, that seemed to them impracticable. Not believing that these Methodist ministers were wicked enough to still the voice which they doubted not, God had bidden to speak, we prefer in charity to believe, they thought God too prudent to commission a black Ambassador. And what was their crime, but acting upon the damnable policy of expediency—of doing what seemed to be necessary, but not just — of compelling the Church, the Church that should account to no man, and to no times, to succumb to the base prejudices of the human heart.

(*b*) Would as many have been ordained? Possibly in proportion to the number, there would have been as many ordained, but in a local capacity. The

THE BLACK PRESS AND THE LAW OF AGITATION

> *"Agitation is the life-blood of all reform movements. It not only lays the foundation, but it builds the superstructure . . . The whole universe is subject to this law . . . Agitation is life; stagnation is death – moral, spiritual and physical death.*
>
> *When truth and error meet each other, their belligerent proclivities are at once developed. There must be war between them in the very nature of things . . . This great truth rushes down upon us with the gathered momentum of all the ages. It cannot be obliterated from the pages of history."* **Rev. George T. Watkins, Baltimore, 1867.**

Dr. Martin R. Delaney of Pittsburgh was one of the leaders of the pre-Civil War period who clearly understood the necessity and the effectiveness of public debate in the promotion of social change. Undaunted by the refusal of the white press in Pittsburgh to publish letters and public addresses expressing interpretation of the issues from the black perspective, Delaney began publication of **The Mystery** in 1843. Delaney was not only a highly respected physician, he was a lecturer, the first black major in the United States Army, a world traveler, a judge, and the "father of black nationalism." The reproduction shown in this book which carried a report on the "great fire" in Pittsburgh is dated Wednesday, April 16, 1845 and may be found in the Pennsylvania Room of the Carnegie Library.

One of the most widely-read of the early black periodicals was **The Colored American,** founded in 1837 by Charles Bennett Ray, a minister who was also an energetic civil rights advocate. The paper, devoted to the interest of the black population, was published weekly in New York City. The November, 1909 edition, reprinted here, discusses the key issues of the day, political disfranchisement and the fight to outlaw lynching.

The page of the January, 1934 edition of **The Crisis** shows a capsule view of issues and events which, with a few changes in the date line, might be mistaken for a look at the world of the 1970's. Edited by one of the greatest scholars America has ever produced, W.E.B. DuBois, the magazine was founded in 1910 as the official instrument of news and commentary for the National Association for the Advancement of Colored People.

The convention movement, the publication of scores of newspapers throughout the nation, and the emergence of new and stronger protest movements, all demonstrate the faith of black Americans in the law of agitation as a means of redress of grievances. The Niagara Movement at Niagara Falls, Canada, convened in 1905, in opposition to the posture of compromise assumed by Booker T. Washington and taken by too many whites as representative of the opinions and feelings of most black Americans. The speaker for the second annual meeting, the Rev. Reverdy C. Ransom, invoked the spirit of John Brown, the willingness to die if necessary, to dramatize the urgency of relentless war against racism and inequality. Though the movement lasted only about five years its leaders and its impact on public policy paved the way for the building of the more forceful and permanent NAACP.

THE M[illegible]STER[illegible].

"And Moses was learned [illegible] wisdom of the Egyptians."—Bible.

[illegible]—No 34 PITTSBURGH, WE[illegible]SDAY MORNING APRIL 16, 1845. [illegible] Price

THE MYSTERY

[illegible] every W[illegible] morning by

THE PUBLISHING COMMITTEE

[illegible] MATTHEW JONES, [illegible] WILLIAMS, PETER BLACKSON, [illegible] J. N. TEMPLETON.

[illegible]—One dollar [illegible] payable in advance; One dollar and twenty-[illegible] cents if not [illegible] within three months; [illegible] One dollar and fifty [illegible] at the end of the year.

RATES OF ADVERTIS[illegible].

Advertisements will [illegible] be inserted at the [illegible] rates per square [illegible] twelve lines—

[illegible] insertion	00 25	Two months	1 00
[illegible] do	00 37[illegible]	Three do	1 50
Three do	00 [illegible]	Six do	2 00
[illegible] do	00 75	Twelve do	3 00

All letters or communications pertaining [illegible] editorial department must be post paid [illegible] to the Editor, those on business to [illegible] of the Publishing Committee."

[illegible] of "THE MYSTERY" can be obtained [illegible] news boys every Wednesday morning, [illegible] at the counter of Mr. Isaac Harris, Intelligence Office, Fifth street, and of M. R. Delany, No. [illegible], Third street, between Wood and Smithfield streets, at the counter of H. Price, confectioner, Allegheny [illegible] at the west end of the Allegheny Bridge. Price two cents.

Agents for the Mystery.

PENNSYLVANIA.

[illegible], George W. Parker, T. Norris, Rev. A. D[illegible] [illegible] B. Vashon.
[illegible]ville, & [illegible], Rev. J J. Clinton, Rev. A. R. [illegible]
[illegible]ville—T. [illegible]
[illegible] A T Hall [illegible]
[illegible], John Molson.
Philadelphia, H. J. Williamson, 31 N 5th st
[illegible]ville, J. Robinson and S. Arnett.
[illegible]town, N. M'Curdy and J. R. Lewis.
[illegible], Fayette county, Alex. Austin.
Monongahela city, Washg. co., Wm. Ralph.
[illegible] Allegheny [illegible]
[illegible] County [illegible] Fayette Davis and [illegible]
[illegible]
East Bethlehem, Ephra[illegible] Arnett.
[illegible]town, D. Canyo[illegible]
Waynesburg Wm. McCurdy.
Allegheny city, Jos[illegible] Mahorney, E. R. [illegible] Parker, Rev Abra[illegible] Cole.
Hollidaysburg, Wm. N[illegible]bit and D. Williams.
[illegible]ville, Joseph Curti[illegible]
Canonsburg, F L. Chambers and D. Arnet.
Harrisburg, C. J. Dorr[illegible]
[illegible], P. O. Allegheny Co. C H Little.

OHIO.

Sandusky city, John [illegible]t.
Cleveland, Robinson & Davis.
[illegible], J. S. Thompson.
[illegible], T. E. Rona.
Columbus, Joseph B[illegible]nnet and G. W. Stanton.
[illegible]ville, T. H [illegible]ett.
Chillicothe, R. R. Chancellor and C. H. Lang[illegible]ton.
Portsmouth, [illegible]
Zanesville, W[illegible]am B. Messer, and [illegible] W. Gar[illegible]
[illegible] Creek, [illegible] Esq., P. M.
New Athens, [illegible]well, Esq., P. M.
[illegible]ville, [illegible], S. Malbury and W. [illegible] Farns.
[illegible], N[illegible]
Cincinnati, [illegible], John I. Gaines and [illegible] W. D. [illegible]
[illegible], [illegible], Griffin J. Watson.
[illegible] Colle[illegible] [illegible]e B. Vashon.
[illegible], [illegible], Jeffrey Day.
[illegible] [illegible]ANA.
[illegible]ville, [illegible]

Local News.

City Subscribers.

Those of our city subscribers [illegible] ved on the First of April, will ple[illegible] us notice of their new place [illegible] and those who have been thr[illegible] by the late calamity, we shall [illegible] as it is possible for us to find the[illegible] of course, it will take some ti[illegible] to get located in anything like perm[illegible]tions.

Mr. Matthew Jones, Barber and Hair Dresser, requests us to [illegible] his Customers and the citizens [illegible]ally, that he has repaired up his h[illegible] and is now carrying on business as [illegible] the old stand in Fourth st. bet[illegible] Wood and Market.

Mr. John Peck, Orna[illegible] Hair Manufacturer, being amon[illegible] who fortunately escaped the drea[illegible] [illegible]ster, is still in his old stand on [illegible]street, next door to the United St[illegible] now the Bank of Pittsburgh.

Injustice.

It has been somewhat [illegible] reported, that Mr. Joseph Mahon[illegible] Jr., residing on Coal Lane, is now [illegible] prison for stolen goods found in [illegible], taken at the great fire. This [illegible] [illegible]ly authorized by his lady to [illegible] [illegible]founded, and utterly false, Mr. [illegible] being [illegible]

[illegible] derson, who makes [illegible] at Mrs. Mahoney's, which wer[illegible] by some persons, carried to t[illegible] the New Court house, exposed [illegible], and returned to Mrs. Ande[illegible] [illegible] her lodgings at Mrs. Mahon[illegible]

This report, we a[illegible], was raised by some treache[illegible] person, who informed the offic[illegible] searching the house, that suc[illegible] were to be found on Mr. Mah[illegible]ouses, not knowing but what [illegible] home.—Such persons, must b[illegible] themselves, or they would no[illegible] others.

Lo[illegible]

Samuel Kingston, [illegible]y at Law Second st., Mrs. Su[illegible] Washerwoman, Third st., M[illegible]. Auction dealer who resided [illegible]heny city, and a servant girl of [illegible]ston, have been lost in the destru[illegible]ents.

[illegible]

ish. Let us lay our eyes to work, and cultivate the soil of our minds; our intellects are good but they need much cultivation; we must unite as one household, the faithful part of our people unite together in praye[illegible] to God as Moses did, when he was pleading for his people. We know we are an oppressed people, and i[illegible] we don't use our own means to fetc[illegible] us out of this estate of misery and o[illegible]pression we never may expect to be a people.

Let us begin now and say with[illegible] ourselves we will not be scoffed at any more on the account of:—n[illegible] color, but condition; we must u[illegible] together as one family not havi[illegible] any self or animosity with it. [illegible] then we will soon see the sons [illegible] daughters of Ham coming up ou[illegible] the Wilderness and crying as th[illegible] go along, Equality! Equality!!

But before this is done we [illegible] have to reform our walk and [illegible] our conversation, and it become[illegible] as females in all of our deportm[illegible] to act what we profess.

We must work for ourselves [illegible] that with all our might, we must do it with meekness, humility and s[illegible]ty. Not boasting for our comp[illegible]cy above others, but let us join [illegible] and heart together, believing that [illegible] we send up our voices together, [illegible] the Lord will say as he said to Moses; "I have heard the cry of m[illegible]ple. I will go down and de[illegible] them from bondage." We nee[illegible] not tell you that faith and charity [illegible] wanting amongst us, we mus[illegible] judges of our own matters [illegible] and by so doing we [illegible] say to our oppressors, [illegible] to Jonadab "if thy heart is r[illegible] my heart, as my heart is w[illegible] give me thy hand" and then [illegible] will join hands with his oppr[illegible] proclaim, Liberty! Liber[illegible] Equality with all Mankind.

For the [illegible]

Philadelphia Correspondence

Friend M. R. Delany.—Until recently, I have not seen or known much of the doings of the citizens of Pittsburgh. A kind friend of mine was good enough to supply me with the Mystery. I have been pleased from the fact th[illegible] a goodly number of acquainta[illegible] our city, and I am only sorry th[illegible]ple are not more acquainted wit[illegible]h other in things that pertain t[illegible]ce and welfare. We are living [illegible]ge age of the world's history, a[illegible]h surrounded with all the inst[illegible] that [illegible]

[illegible]; when we contra[illegible] [illegible] we have reason [illegible] [illegible] blessings so abundent[illegible] [illegible] If our people w[illegible] [illegible] their situation and use e[illegible] [illegible] themselves, there [illegible] [illegible] state of things in [illegible] [illegible] Where we now see mis[illegible] [illegible] happiness, comfor[illegible] Philadelphia we have had [illegible] the subject of slavery [illegible] people, than we ever [illegible] probability. The '[illegible] thieves,' and the 'testimo[illegible] [illegible]esses' sold by our E[illegible] [illegible] been read very ex[illegible] [illegible] to a good purpose, for [illegible]wledged that we lean [illegible] [illegible]h to sanction the colon[illegible] Only a few years ago I saw [illegible] paper, a Biographical sket[illegible] [illegible] distinguished ministe[illegible] [illegible] the writer has taken [illegible] state that he though a [illegible] [illegible] an abolitionest, but [illegible] the colonization scheme! [illegible] sidered one of his good q[illegible] others similar: how then [illegible] to elevate ourselves while [illegible] or support that accurse[illegible] is high time that our actio[illegible] abolition. 'Faith without [illegible] The most of us are Abo[illegible] but not in action.

I see by the papers, [illegible] human rights in Ohio are [illegible]

[illegible]

[illegible] our determinations kn[illegible] countenance or support [illegible]

Yo[illegible]

Philadelphia, Mar. [illegible]

For [illegible]

Pittsburgh, Pa

Brother M. R. Delan[illegible]

By your permissio[illegible], would respectfully inf[illegible] to the Manual Labor S[illegible] that the land contracted [illegible] session, and rented [illegible] Thos. Lawrence informs [illegible] dated Columbus, Ohio. Thus, we have struggle[illegible] our first payments &c.

Yours respectfully, a[illegible] above.

M. J. W[illegible]

To Ag[illegible]

THE COLORED AMERICAN MAGAZINE

VOL. XVII. NOVEMBER, 1909 NO. 5

THE MONTH

The past month has been one of significant and portentous things for the Negro. Forward among these was the election on November 2. On that day it may be said was fulfilled the prophecy of the late Senator Hoar, of Massachusetts, to the effect the boundaries of disfranchisement would be coterminous with those of the Confederacy.

POLITICAL

The disfranchising constitution amendment, under which the Democratic organization expected to shut out 50,000 Negro voters in Maryland, was defeated Tuesday, November 2, by a majority of 5,000 to 6,000. The Legislature will be Democratic in both branches, insuring the re-election of United States Senator Rayner.

Four years ago an amendment similar to the one defeated, though more drastic in its provisions, was rejected by 34,058 majority. At that time Governor Warfield and his following of Democrats, together with the entire independent vote, were against the amendment. A large proportion of the Warfield element voted for the amendment.

The vote in some of the strongly Democratic counties was not as heavy for the amendment as had been expected. The western section of the State rolled up its usual Republican majority. Hundreds of ballots which represented votes against the amendment were thrown out in the eastern and southern counties, in which trick ballots were used. These ballots were so confusing that few men excepting Democrats who were posted beforehand could mark them intelligently. Some of these ballots were four or five feet long, without any party designations, and the names of the various candidates were mixed to trick the voter.

FEDERAL BLOW AT LYNCHING

Hardly less significant than this decisive defeat of disfranchisement was the remarkable decision against Sheriff Shipp, of Chattanooga, in the lynching case.

Joseph F. Shipp, sheriff, his deputy, Jeremiah Gibson, who was the jailer,

THE CRISIS

Founded 1910
REG. U. S. PAT. OFF

A Record of the Darker Races

W. E. Burghardt Du Bois, *Editor* — **George W. Streator, *Acting Business Manager***

Volume 41, *No.* 1 — *Whole No.* 278

Contents for January, 1934

THE CRISIS FOR FEBRUARY

This month we are publishing timely articles on the New Deal and American Dollar Imperialism. Next month we will go further into these questions, presenting other points of view that are gaining currency. THE CRISIS believes more than ever before that there is a need for clear and brave thinking on problems and programs affecting the darker world. In addition, THE CRISIS will continue to encourage fiction and poetry.

AS THE CROW FLIES

It has taken just 157 years for a President of the United States to say in plain English that lynching is "a vile form of collective murder."

•

What we need is not more money nor less; not a gold standard or a silver standard; not higher prices or lower prices; but the abolition of private profit as the main basis of industry.

•

The secret of Lindbergh's success is neither dumb luck nor extraordinary skill; but infinite capacity for taking pains beforehand.

•

It is possible that the same gentleman who killed Cock Robin may be responsible for the death of the League of Nations.

•

When is a free and independent nation neither independent nor free? When it belongs to the British Empire, says Ireland.

•

We may yet be able to date the fall of Hitler in Germany at the disfranchisement of German women.

•

Which brings us to remark that every statesman who yells about Children, Church and Kitchen, ought to be made to bear twins, to listen to as many sermons as we have, and to wash dishes and diapers for at least ten years.

•

Inborn culture manifests itself in characteristic ways; in time of stress, England rallies around the income of the Aristocracy; France overthrows the Cabinet to keep down taxes; and the United States stages a lynching to appease the morons.

•

The United States despite itself is compelled to play the old game at Montevideo: America for all, providing the U.S.A. is America; no intervention, except in Cuba; no public collection of private debt, except in Haiti; the Monroe Doctrine forever in the interests of Monroe's country.

•

Now that liquor is here, what of it?

•

Spain has lurched to the Right and is trying to outlaw the Left. The last revolution was too easy to last, and now it must all be done again. The Grandees and the Clergy stand arrayed in the old battle against Labor and Poverty.

•

And so Mr. Litvinoff, with the stars and stripes protruding from his upper, left-hand coat pocket, thumbed his nose at Berlin, waved a greeting toward Rome, and landed in Moscow.

•

The Chase Bank did what all the other big banks did during the boom, only it did a little more of it. And now what are we doing to do about it? Nothing.

•

Ex-President Dawes' Chicago bank got ninety nice little millions from the government's pocket and has repaid thirty; the rest is now due "on demand." Hell and Maria! Fill up the old pipe and demand be damned!

•

The Women of the World got a pat on the back at Montevideo, but the American ladies could only get together on bridge rules.

THE CRISIS *was founded in* 1910. *It is published monthly at* 69 *Fifth Avenue, New York, N. Y., by Crisis Publishing Company, Inc., and is the official organ of the National Association for the Advancement of Colored People. The subscription price is* $1.50 *a year or* 15c *a copy. Foreign subscriptions* $1.75. *The date of expiration of each subscription is printed on the wrapper. When the subscription is due a blue renewal blank is enclosed. The address of a subscriber may be changed as often as desired, but both the old and new address must be given and two weeks' notice is necessary. Manuscripts and drawings relating to colored people are desired. They must be accompanied by return postage, and while* THE CRISIS *uses every care it assumes no responsibility for their safety in transit. Entered as second class matter November* 2, 1910, *at the post office at New York, N. Y., under the act of March* 3, 1879, *and additional second class entry at Albany, N. Y.*

The Spirit of John Brown

A Speech Delivered by Rev. Reverdy C. Ransom, D. of Boston, Mass., before the Second Annual Meeting of The Niagara Movement

HARPER'S FERRY, W. VA., AUGUST 17, 1906

Great epochs in the world's his ory are hinged upon some spot of lan or sea, which becomes historic and sacred forever more. There are Mt. Sinai and Mt. Calvary, the Jordan, the Euphrates, the Nile and Rubi on, Thermopylae, Runnymede, Water oo, Gettysburg, Appomatox, Port Ar hur and Manila Bay; WHILE JOHN BROWN HAS MADE HARPER'S FERRY AS CLASSIC AS BUNKER HILL.

The leonine soul of this old hero-saint and martyr proves how impotent and defenseless are tyranny, injustice and wrong, even when upheld by the sanction of the law, suppo ed by the power of money and defen ed by the sword.

If modern history furnishes a s litary example of he appearance o a man who possess d the spirit of he prophets of ancient Israel, it is J Brown. The sublime courage w which he met the Goliath of slav in mortal combat, was not surpas by that of David, who went forth meet the Philistine who had de the a mies of the living God. He v commissioned by the same author and bore the same credentials as Moses, who left his flocks in Midian Desert to go and stand bef Pharoah and demand in the name "I Am That I Am" that he sho free his slaves.

John Brown left his flocks fields at Mt. Elba, New York fought at Osawatomie to make the of Kansas free; at Harper's Fe where his brave followers fought fell, he delivered a blow agai slavery in the most vital part, fired the gun whose opening echoed the sound of the death k of slavery.

FREEDOM OBTAINED, THE BATTLE FOR EQUALITY STILL RAGES

Freedom came officially with the adoption of the Thirteenth Amendment to the Constitution in 1865. The Fourteenth Amendment granting citizenship was added in 1868 and the Fifteenth Amendment, extended the right to vote in 1870, except for women, white and black.

The promise of radical reconstruction, however, fell far short of expectation. Civil rights laws were written and nullified within a few years. Twenty-two blacks served in the national Congress and some held high offices in state and local government, but these gains were short lived. The "Compromise of 1877" marked the withdrawal of federal protection for black voters. Emboldened by the "Atlanta Compromise" of 1895, the Supreme Court legalized racism with the 1896 decision, *Plessy* vs. *Ferguson*. Lynch mobs carried on a wave of terror and bigots vowed to keep the Negro politically impotent and economically impoverished.

Blacks fought against this denial of their basic humanity using a variety of methods. Their responses to oppression included migration to the North and to the cities, the founding of church-supported schools and colleges, the organization of multiple self-help societies. Recognizing the need for economic freedom, some established banks, insurance companies and numerous small businesses. A few received political appointments to middle level federal offices, but generally speaking, a share in the national abundance was deliberately and effectively withheld from the black minority.

The general will was clearly expressed in terms of second-class citizenship and perpetual denial of opportunity for black people. Equality was a word which few Americans appeared to understand.

As John Hope Franklin argues so forcefully in an essay published during the national bicentennial celebration, the nature of equality is such that it cannot be divided. He writes:

> *"More than anything else, however, Americans of every race, creed, economic rank, and social position need to recognize that equality is indeed indivisible. For the entire life of this nation an effort has been made to divide equality — to create a social order in which equality was to be enjoyed by some on the basis of race and denied to others because they did not belong to that race — and it has not worked."* *

* John Hope Franklin, **Racial Equality in America**, Chicago, 1976, pp. 107, 108.

A LEGACY OF LEADERSHIP

Mary McLeod Bethune
1875-1955

Asa Philip Randolph
1889-1979

Afro-Americans became increasingly militant in the early decades of the twentieth century especially after they had closed ranks and fought in World War I to make the world safe for Democracy.

During the 1920's, the era of the new Negro and the Harlem Renaissance, blacks began to rethink their political affiliation and concluded that their support of parties and candidates should be based squarely on self-interest. It was generally agreed that whatever debt they owed the Republican Party had been paid in full and an overwhelming majority transferred their votes to the party of Franklin Delano Roosevelt who offered them a New Deal to ease the pain of the Great Depression.

The Congressional record of July 9, 1936 listed six "firsts" claimed by the Democratic party and the Hon. James L. Quinn of Pennsylvania called attention to Executive Order 7036 which created the National Youth Administration. Mrs. Mary McLeod Bethune, founder of Bethune--Cookman College in Floriaa and pioneer of the National Council of Negro Women, and Dr. Mordecai Johnson, president of Howard University, were named to the national advisory committee. Later, President Roosevelt appointed Mrs. Bethune as Director of Negro Affairs for NYA. With Mrs. Bethune, other prominent blacks, including Ralph Bunche, William Hastie and Robert Weaver, formed the influential "Black Cabinet" of the Roosevelt years.

The following news story was published in Negro newspapers throughout the country following the Democratic National Convention in Philadelphia, June 23–27, 1936.

DEMOCRATIC FIRSTS

1. First to institute Negro Press Conference.
2. First to seat a Negro woman as a regular delegate to a major-party convention.
3. First to seat a Negro in the general press box.
4. First to open convention with invocation by Negro.
5. First time in history to seat 10 delegates and 22 alternates (Negro).
6. [illegible]st time a Negro addressed a convention (Congressman MITCHELL, of Illinois).

roads. It was only a few years after the prosperous ones got automobiles until they were quite a few in number. As more people got automobiles, the demand for better roads grew. Today almost everone in Upper Turkeyfoot Township and other parts of the district own some kind of an automobile, and in some cases two or three.

Mr. Speaker, I mention these settings for one purpose only. They vividly paint the picture of how we adjust ourselves from time to time as a people to keep pace with the ever-increasing adjustments in the business world and the social world around us.

It was not necessary in those buckwagon days and dump-

once again, I declare that the American people are not so credulous and gullible.

Governor Landon in March of 1933 also said:

> I desire to acknowledge in a tangible way the appreciation of the people of my State for the courage with which Roosevelt has tackled the depression.

And the Cleveland platform declares the administration "has bred fear and hesitation in commerce and industry."

Again in May of 1934 Governor Landon said:

> It would be good business, in my opinion, for Kansas to borrow every dollar it can get under the P. W. A. that could possibly be spent on highway work by July 1935.

And the Republican platform says, "The New Deal administration constantly seeks to usurp the rights reserved to the States and the people" and "it has destroyed the morale of our people and made them dependent upon government."

And in September of 1934 Governor Landon, not then the Presidential nominee of his party, said:

> We have not yet found how to control and manage the industrial civilization which we have created. The only way we can find the solution is the age-old way of trial and error and experience.

Even as late as November 1935 Governor Landon said:

> I am confident that the President and the W. P. A. are doing all in their power to get the people to work.

And the Republican platform declares the Roosevelt administration "has bred fear and hesitation in commerce, thus discouraging new enterprises, preventing employment, and prolonging the depression."

What a change has come over the Governor of Kansas who has become the Republican nominee for the Presidency. Now Republican Presidential nominee, Alfred Mossman Landon, says, "The centralization of control in Washington has brought about a lamentable break-down of local responsibility", and that the Roosevelt administration "has made the worst record ever made in the history of the United States in bringing this country out of a depression."

And finally Governor Landon declares:

> If we, as Republicans, would keep faith with the people, our platform must say exactly what we mean—and we must mean exactly what our platform says.

What did Governor Landon mean as Governor of Kansas, and what does he mean as the Republican candidate for President?

It is of interest to note that most of the pro-Roosevelt utterances by Governor Landon were made in 1934. Landon was a candidate for Governor. Can there be any doubt that his campaign, particularly his stressing a major part of the Roosevelt policies of recovery, played a large part in his election as the Republican Governor?

Let me call your attention to the latest evidence as to how the Old Guard is working with Governor Landon in his quest for public office. Governor Landon has announced that among his advisers who will shape his speeches during the campaign is Charles P. Taft, brother of Robert Taft and son of a former Republican Old Guard President. Frederick T. Robey, economist of the Columbia University, who writes a column on economics for the New York Herald Tribune, a

Hoover, Ogden Mills, Walter Brown, Jouett Shouse, of the Liberty League, Charles Dewey Hilles, contact man for Wall Street, Jim Watson, the Du Ponts, and a score of others take to the open spaces of America and from the agricultural platform speak in his behalf for the greatest office within the gift of the American people?

The Roosevelt New Deal and the Colored Citizen

EXTENSION OF REMARKS

OF

HON. JAMES L. QUINN

OF PENNSYLVANIA

IN THE HOUSE OF REPRESENTATIVES

Wednesday, June 3, 1936

Mr. QUINN. Mr. Speaker, President Roosevelt in a recent speech said:

> There are none of us who do not hope that our children get a better break than we had. * * * We want them to have an opportunity for profitable character building—decent, wholesome living—good work and good play.

This statement is exemplary of the inclusiveness of the spirit and practice of the Roosevelt New Deal administration.

June 26, 1935, by Executive Order 7036, the President created the National Youth Administration. August 1, 1935, Mrs. Mary McLeod Bethune, of Daytona, Fla., for many years one of the leading educators of the colored race, and Dr. Mordecai W. Johnson, president of Howard University, Washington, D. C., were appointed as members of the N. Y. A. national advisory committee by the President.

April 29, 1936, in the drawing room of the White House from 9 p. m. until nearly midnight, President Roosevelt sat down with the members of the N. Y. A. national advisory committee to review at first hand the phenomenal progress made to date in this new social endeavor.

Aubrey Williams, the inspired genius and executive secretary of the N. Y. A., presented each member of the committee to the President. In her turn Mrs. Bethune recited the accomplishments of the colored youth as reflected in the statistical records of the organization, which were in brief as follows:

Twenty-eight colored leaders are members of the State N. Y. A. advisory committees, North and South. An equal number of colored assistant State directors and trained college men and women of the colored race are filling high executive positions in New York, Pennsylvania, Florida, Virginia, Kentucky, Illinois, Tennessee, Indiana, Ohio, Missouri, Michigan, Kansas, Georgia, Colorado, California, and Texas, which State programs have had the largest participation of young colored men and women.

The National Youth Administration is helping approximately 26,000 colored youth to continue in school through payments for part-time work under supervision of school authorities. These young people range in age from 16 to 25

FOR IMMEDIATE RELEASE MAY 17, 1979

Office of the White House Press Secretary

THE WHITE HOUSE

STATEMENT BY THE PRESIDENT

It can be said of few individuals in our time that they helped transform the face of the American nation. A. Philip Randolph was one of those giants. His leadership in the trade union and civil rights movements has left an indelible mark on almost every area of our national life. A. Philip Randolph helped sweep away long standing barriers of discrimination and segregation in industry and labor unions, in our schools and armed services, in politics and government.

For each new generation of civil rights leaders, he was an inspiration and an example. His dignity and integrity, his eloquence, his devotion to non-violence, and his unshakeable commitment to justice all helped shape the ideals and spirit of the civil rights movement.

His voice and inspiration will long be missed, but America will always be a more just, more humane, and more decent nation because A. Philip Randolph lived among us.

When President Jimmy Carter delivered the May 1979 commencement address at historic Cheyney State College in Philadelphia, he paid high tribute to the life and works of a twentieth century giant, A. Philip Randolph who died that week. It was Randolph who fathered the March on Washington movement which captured the hearts of generations of Americans who have yearned for true egalitarianism.

In 1917 he challenged the power structure urging civil disobedience to protest bias in the armed forces. He published the radical paper, **The Messenger**, in the 1920's and later organized the first strong black labor union, the Brotherhood of Sleeping Car Porters. In 1941 it was Randolph who designed the bold plan to bring tens of thousands of black marchers to the nation's capital in order to dramatize the inconsistency of fighting against fascism abroad while blatant racism was tolerated at home. His forthright, courageous leadership brought together a determined coalition of organizations which persuaded President Roosevelt to issue Executive Order 8802 on June 25, 1941. He was also the prime mover in the campaign which resulted in the proclamation of Executive Order 9981 by President Harry Truman on July 26, 1948 outlawing discrimination in the armed forces.

Mrs. Bethune and A. Philip Randolph were committed leaders of high purpose and vision. Both lived to see some of their dreams come true but neither of them ever retreated from the firing line until they faced the unbeatable foe — death.

SELECTED BIBLIOGRAPHY

The African Repository and Colonial Journal, Vol. XI, Washington, D.C., 1835.

Delaney, Martin R., **The Condition, Elevation, Emigration and Destiny of the Colored People of the United States**, Philadelphia, 1852.

Fishel, Leslie H., Jr. and Quarles, Benjamin, eds., **The Negro American: A Documentary History**, Glenview, Ill., 1967.

Franklin, John Hope, **Racial Equality in America**, Chicago, 1976.

Frazier, E. Franklin, **The Negro Church in America**, University of Liverpool, 1963.

George, Carol V.R., **Segregated Sabbaths, Richard Allen and the Rise of Independent Black Churches**, 1760 - 1840, New York, 1973.

Henson, Josiah, **Father Henson's Story of His Own Life**, Boston, 1858.

Higginson, Thomas Wentworth, **Army Life in a Black Regiment**, Boston, 1870.

Holland, Frederick May, **Frederick Douglass: The Colored Orator**, New York, 1895.

Huggins, Nathan, et. al., eds., **Key Issues in the Afro-American Experience**, 2 vols., New York, 1971.

Lundy, Benjamin, **The Life, Travels and Opinions of Benjamin Lundy**, Philadelphia, 1847.

Penn, I. Garland, **The Afro-American Press and Its Editors**, Springfield, Mass., 1861; reprint Arno Press, New York, 1969.

Proceedings of the National Convention, Rochester, 1853.

Proceedings of the National Convention of Colored Men, Syracuse, 1864.

Proceedings of the State Convention of the Colored Freemen of Pennsylvania, Pittsburgh, 1841.

Quarles, Benjamin, **Black Abolitionists**, New York, 1969.

Richings, G.F., **Evidences of Progress Among Colored People**, Philadelphia, 1903.

Rogers, Joel A., **Africa's Gift to America**, New York, 1961.

Samkange, Stanlake, **The African Saga**, New York, 1971.

Stowe, Harriet Beecher, **Key to Uncle Tom's Cabin**, Boston, 1853.

Tanner, Benjamin Tucker, **Apology for African Methodism**, Baltimore, 1867.

Walker, Jonathan, **The Branded Hand**, Boston, 1846.

Woodson, Carter G., **The History of the Negro Church**, Associated Publishers, Washington, D.C. 1921.

Books of Related Interest

THE BLACK MAN IN WHITE AMERICA
by John G. Van Deusen

THE HISTORY OF THE NEGRO CHURCH
by Carter G. Woodson

MIS-EDUCATION OF THE NEGRO
by Carter G. Woodson

THE NEGRO IN OUR HISTORY
by Carter G. Woodson, revised by Charles H. Wesley

HARRIET TUBMAN
by Earl Conrad

WOMEN BUILDERS
by Sadie Iola Daniel, revised and enlarged by Thelma D. Perry and Charles H. Wesley